Dangerous positions and proceedings published and practised vvithin this iland of Britaine, under pretence of reformation, and for the presbyteriall discipline. Collected, and set forth by Richard Bancroft ... (1640)

Richard Bancroft

Dangerous positions and proceedings published and practised vvithin this iland of Britaine, under pretence of reformation, and for the presbyteriall discipline. Collected, and set forth by Richard Bancroft ...
Bancroft, Richard, 1544-1610.
A line-for-line resetting of the 1593 edition ending on leaf Aa4.
[8], 183, [1] p.
London : Printed by R. Young and R. Badger, Anno 1640.
STC (2nd ed.) / 1345
English
Reproduction of the original in the Cambridge University Library

Early English Books Online (EEBO) Editions

Imagine holding history in your hands.

Now you can. Digitally preserved and previously accessible only through libraries as Early English Books Online, this rare material is now available in single print editions. Thousands of books written between 1475 and 1700 and ranging from religion to astronomy, medicine to music, can be delivered to your doorstep in individual volumes of high-quality historical reproductions.

We have been compiling these historic treasures for more than 70 years. Long before such a thing as "digital" even existed, ProQuest founder Eugene Power began the noble task of preserving the British Museum's collection on microfilm. He then sought out other rare and endangered titles, providing unparalleled access to these works and collaborating with the world's top academic institutions to make them widely available for the first time. This project furthers that original vision.

These texts have now made the full journey -- from their original printing-press versions available only in rare-book rooms to online library access to new single volumes made possible by the partnership between artifact preservation and modern printing technology. A portion of the proceeds from every book sold supports the libraries and institutions that made this collection possible, and that still work to preserve these invaluable treasures passed down through time.

This is history, traveling through time since the dawn of printing to your own personal library.

Initial Proquest EEBO Print Editions collections include:

Early Literature

This comprehensive collection begins with the famous Elizabethan Era that saw such literary giants as Chaucer, Shakespeare and Marlowe, as well as the introduction of the sonnet. Traveling through Jacobean and Restoration literature, the highlight of this series is the Pollard and Redgrave 1475-1640 selection of the rarest works from the English Renaissance.

Early Documents of World History

This collection combines early English perspectives on world history with documentation of Parliament records, royal decrees and military documents that reveal the delicate balance of Church and State in early English government. For social historians, almanacs and calendars offer insight into daily life of common citizens. This exhaustively complete series presents a thorough picture of history through the English Civil War.

Historical Almanacs

Historically, almanacs served a variety of purposes from the more practical, such as planting and harvesting crops and plotting nautical routes, to predicting the future through the movements of the stars. This collection provides a wide range of consecutive years of "almanacks" and calendars that depict a vast array of everyday life as it was several hundred years ago.

Early History of Astronomy & Space

Humankind has studied the skies for centuries, seeking to find our place in the universe. Some of the most important discoveries in the field of astronomy were made in these texts recorded by ancient stargazers, but almost as impactful were the perspectives of those who considered their discoveries to be heresy. Any independent astronomer will find this an invaluable collection of titles arguing the truth of the cosmic system.

Early History of Industry & Science

Acting as a kind of historical Wall Street, this collection of industry manuals and records explores the thriving industries of construction; textile, especially wool and linen; salt; livestock; and many more.

Early English Wit, Poetry & Satire

The power of literary device was never more in its prime than during this period of history, where a wide array of political and religious satire mocked the status quo and poetry called humankind to transcend the rigors of daily life through love, God or principle. This series comments on historical patterns of the human condition that are still visible today.

Early English Drama & Theatre

This collection needs no introduction, combining the works of some of the greatest canonical writers of all time, including many plays composed for royalty such as Queen Elizabeth I and King Edward VI. In addition, this series includes history and criticism of drama, as well as examinations of technique.

Early History of Travel & Geography

Offering a fascinating view into the perception of the world during the sixteenth and seventeenth centuries, this collection includes accounts of Columbus's discovery of the Americas and encompasses most of the Age of Discovery, during which Europeans and their descendants intensively explored and mapped the world. This series is a wealth of information from some the most groundbreaking explorers.

Early Fables & Fairy Tales

This series includes many translations, some illustrated, of some of the most well-known mythologies of today, including Aesop's Fables and English fairy tales, as well as many Greek, Latin and even Oriental parables and criticism and interpretation on the subject.

Early Documents of Language & Linguistics

The evolution of English and foreign languages is documented in these original texts studying and recording early philology from the study of a variety of languages including Greek, Latin and Chinese, as well as multilingual volumes, to current slang and obscure words. Translations from Latin, Hebrew and Aramaic, grammar treatises and even dictionaries and guides to translation make this collection rich in cultures from around the world.

Early History of the Law

With extensive collections of land tenure and business law "forms" in Great Britain, this is a comprehensive resource for all kinds of early English legal precedents from feudal to constitutional law, Jewish and Jesuit law, laws about public finance to food supply and forestry, and even "immoral conditions." An abundance of law dictionaries, philosophy and history and criticism completes this series.

Early History of Kings, Queens and Royalty

This collection includes debates on the divine right of kings, royal statutes and proclamations, and political ballads and songs as related to a number of English kings and queens, with notable concentrations on foreign rulers King Louis IX and King Louis XIV of France, and King Philip II of Spain. Writings on ancient rulers and royal tradition focus on Scottish and Roman kings, Cleopatra and the Biblical kings Nebuchadnezzar and Solomon.

Early History of Love, Marriage & Sex

Human relationships intrigued and baffled thinkers and writers well before the postmodern age of psychology and self-help. Now readers can access the insights and intricacies of Anglo-Saxon interactions in sex and love, marriage and politics, and the truth that lies somewhere in between action and thought.

Early History of Medicine, Health & Disease

This series includes fascinating studies on the human brain from as early as the 16th century, as well as early studies on the physiological effects of tobacco use. Anatomy texts, medical treatises and wound treatment are also discussed, revealing the exponential development of medical theory and practice over more than two hundred years.

Early History of Logic, Science and Math

The "hard sciences" developed exponentially during the 16th and 17th centuries, both relying upon centuries of tradition and adding to the foundation of modern application, as is evidenced by this extensive collection. This is a rich collection of practical mathematics as applied to business, carpentry and geography as well as explorations of mathematical instruments and arithmetic; logic and logicians such as Aristotle and Socrates; and a number of scientific disciplines from natural history to physics.

Early History of Military, War and Weaponry

Any professional or amateur student of war will thrill at the untold riches in this collection of war theory and practice in the early Western World. The Age of Discovery and Enlightenment was also a time of great political and religious unrest, revealed in accounts of conflicts such as the Wars of the Roses.

Early History of Food

This collection combines the commercial aspects of food handling, preservation and supply to the more specific aspects of canning and preserving, meat carving, brewing beer and even candy-making with fruits and flowers, with a large resource of cookery and recipe books. Not to be forgotten is a "the great eater of Kent," a study in food habits.

Early History of Religion

From the beginning of recorded history we have looked to the heavens for inspiration and guidance. In these early religious documents, sermons, and pamphlets, we see the spiritual impact on the lives of both royalty and the commoner. We also get insights into a clergy that was growing ever more powerful as a political force. This is one of the world's largest collections of religious works of this type, revealing much about our interpretation of the modern church and spirituality.

Early Social Customs

Social customs, human interaction and leisure are the driving force of any culture. These unique and quirky works give us a glimpse of interesting aspects of day-to-day life as it existed in an earlier time. With books on games, sports, traditions, festivals, and hobbies it is one of the most fascinating collections in the series.

The BiblioLife Network

This project was made possible in part by the BiblioLife Network (BLN), a project aimed at addressing some of the huge challenges facing book preservationists around the world. The BLN includes libraries, library networks, archives, subject matter experts, online communities and library service providers. We believe every book ever published should be available as a high-quality print reproduction; printed on-demand anywhere in the world. This insures the ongoing accessibility of the content and helps generate sustainable revenue for the libraries and organizations that work to preserve these important materials.

The following book is in the "public domain" and represents an authentic reproduction of the text as printed by the original publisher. While we have attempted to accurately maintain the integrity of the original work, there are sometimes problems with the original work or the micro-film from which the books were digitized. This can result in minor errors in reproduction. Possible imperfections include missing and blurred pages, poor pictures, markings and other reproduction issues beyond our control. Because this work is culturally important, we have made it available as part of our commitment to protecting, preserving, and promoting the world's literature.

GUIDE TO FOLD-OUTS MAPS and OVERSIZED IMAGES

The book you are reading was digitized from microfilm captured over the past thirty to forty years. Years after the creation of the original microfilm, the book was converted to digital files and made available in an online database.

In an online database, page images do not need to conform to the size restrictions found in a printed book. When converting these images back into a printed bound book, the page sizes are standardized in ways that maintain the detail of the original. For large images, such as fold-out maps, the original page image is split into two or more pages

Guidelines used to determine how to split the page image follows:

- Some images are split vertically; large images require vertical and horizontal splits.
- For horizontal splits, the content is split left to right.
- For vertical splits, the content is split from top to bottom.
- For both vertical and horizontal splits, the image is processed from top left to bottom right.

DANGEROUS POSITIONS AND PROCEEDINGS,

PUBLISHED

AND PRACTISED
VVITHIN THIS ILAND
of BRITAINE, under pretence of
Reformation, and for the
Presbyteriall Discipline.

Collected, and set forth by *Richard Bancroft*, Doctor in Divinity, then Lord Bishop of London, and afterwards Lord Archbishop of Canterbury.

Prov. 24.21. *My sonne, feare thou the Lord, and the King, and meddle not with them that are given to change.*
Jud. *They despise government, and speake evill of dignities.*

Δεινὰ τὰ τῶν τυράννων λήμματα.

LONDON,
Printed by R. *Young* and R. *Badger*. Anno 1640.

Academiæ Cantabrigiensis Liber

424.98

An advertisement to the Reader.

THE Author of this Treatise was required by some persons of honour, who might dispose of him and his labours, to set downe by way of an historicall narration what hee had observed touching certaine positions holden, and some enterprises atchieved or undertaken, for recommending and bringing the Presbyteriall Discipline into this Iland of Brittain, under pretence of reformation. The performance of which duty, when he had undertaken and was entred into it, he found the work to grow farre greater upon him, then at the first he did imagine: Insomuch as although in the beginning he verily supposed, that he might easily have contrived his matter into a few sheets of paper, so that as many copies as were to bee disposed, might easily and in very short time have beene written forth, yet by the necessary length of the Discourse, as it fell out, and through his manifold quotations he was constrained, (as the time required) to procure for the better dispatch, that some few copies might bee printed. And albeit there is no meaning that this Treatise (laboured but for the private satisfaction of some few especiall persons) should otherwise continue then as an unpublished copie: yet the writer of it wished to have it signified, that nothing is alledged therein which is not to bee found either in Bookes and Writings published to the view of the world (such as he thinketh will not be disclaimed) or in publicke records, or else is to be shewed under those parties own hands that have beene either the principall procurers, favorers, or dealers in those things whereof hee intreateth. Which asseveration of his thus made, he will be ready (as he saith) God assisting him, to justifie at any time for the satisfaction of such as shall make doubt of it. And doth further protest with all sincerity that hee hath not (willingly) detorted any thing in this whole Discourse, to make either the cause it selfe or the favourers thereof more odious, then their owne words and deeds shall necessarily inferre and enforce against them with all indifferent and considerate Readers. Farewell in Christ.

The contents of the first Booke.

Of two sorts of men that especially disturbe the Church of England, and of the drifts of them both, by way of a Preface. Chap. 1, Fol. 1

Of the course held at *Geneva* for reformation of religion, and of the doctrine which upon that occasion hath beene broached. Chap. 2. Fol. 7.

Of the proceeding of some Scottish Ministers, according to the *Genevian* rules of Reformation. Chap. 3. Fol. 9

How the *Genevian* Doctrine or principle for Reformation, hath been amplified by certaine pretended Reformers in Scotland. Chap. 4, Fol. 14

The objections against the doctrine, reported of in the former chapter with the Consistorian answers unto them. Cha. 5. Fol. 16

The proceedings of certaine Scottish Ministers, according to the grounds mentioned in the two last chapters for setting up of the Consistorian Discipline, and of their urging of our English Disciplinaries to follow their steps. Cha. 6. Fol. 18

The contents of the second Booke.

The Doctrine of certaine English Ministers which they learned at *Geneva*, and published of purpose to have procured the like course for Reformation in England, to that which was in Scotland. Ch. 1. Fol. 34

Our English Disciplinarians doe imitate the Scottish in their desire of the Consistoriall government, saving that they are more bewitched with a kind of dotage after it. Ch. 2. Fol. 41

Our pretended English Reformers doe imitate or rather exceed the Scottish Ministers in reviling and rayling against all that do encounter them. Cha. 3. Fol. 44

The speeches of the said pretended reformers, concerning England, the state, the present reformation and government of the Church. Cha. 4. Fol. 47

Some of their undutifull and Consistorian speeches concerning her Majesty, &c. Cha. 5. Fol. 48

Some of their rayling speeches against the high court of Parliament, and all others generally that do maintaine the present government of the Church of England. Cha. 6. Fol. 50

Some of their Disciplinarian speeches concerning the Lords of her Majesties most honourable privy councell. Ch. 7. Fol. 52

Some of their rayling speeches against the Magistracy in England, the Judges, Lawyers, and lawes both civill and ecclesiasticall. Ch. 8. Fol. 54

Some of the their consistoriall sayings, as touching our Religion, Communion booke, Sacraments and Ceremonies. Cha. 9. Fol. 55

How they doe charge the present government with persecution. Chap. 10. Fol. 56

Some

The Contents.

Some of their Consistorian speeches of the Clergy of England, assembled as occasion hath required, in the Convocation house. cha. 11. Fol. 58

Some of their presbyteriall speeches of the Bishops of England professing the Gospel. Cha. 12. Fol. 58

Some of their uncharitable words against all the Clergy in England generally that mislike their designements. Cha. 13. Fol. 60

Their especiall drift in their said rayling speeches, as outragiously published as if they were meere Jesuites, and peradventure to as dangerous purpose. Cha. 14. Fol. 61

The Contents of the third book.

The practises of certaine English reformers for Discipline, from the yeare 1560 untill the yeare, 1572. cha. 1. Fol. 65

The secret meetings for Discipline, and the matters handled in them here in England from 1572. till 1583. cha. 2. Fol. 67

A forme or booke of Discipline is drawne, and a resolution agreed upon, how far they might proceed for the practise of it, without breaking the peace of our Church. cha. 3. Fol. 69

About the yeare 1583. they fell againe to the practice of their Discipline, and of a Consistorian question. cha. 4. Fol. 73

Their booke of Discipline is reviewed: it was after sent abroad about 1587. it was put in practise in Northamptonshire and many other places. Cha. 5. Fol. 75

A Synod is held at *Coventry*, 1588. many questions are resolved, the booke of Discipline is subscribed unto. cha. 6. Fol. 85

The booke of the pretended Discipline is made perfect at *Cambridge*, certaine Synods are kept, and of their estimation. cha. 7. Fol. 88

Upon some detecting of the premisses some were called into question, they refuse to be examined, all they were charged, which is in effect confessed. ch. 8. Fol. 91

Cartwright is called for by authority, a Synod is held in London, it is there resolved that he shall refuse to be examined upon his oath. cha. 9. Fol. 93

Further proofe for their practise of their Discipline, collected out of the rules of their subscribed book. cha. 10. Fol. 94

Further proofe for their practise of their Discipline out of the articles they subscribed. cha. 11. Fol. 98

It is contested that they agreed to put one point of their book in practise without her Majesties assent, what it is, and of strange names given to children. ch. 12. Fol. 102

A second point of their booke confessed to bee agreed upon, for the practise of it without her Majesties assent. cha. 13. Fol. 105

Moe points of their booke put in practice: fasts, calling of Ministers, presbyterie, censures, &c. cha. 14. Fol. 112

They have joyned themselves into an association or brotherhood, and doe appropriate to their meetings the name of the Church. cha. 15. Fol. 120

A ridiculous pretence of lawes, with a capitulation of the summe of this third booke. cha. 16. Fol. 125

The contents of the fourth Booke.

Some of them seem to grow desperate, and propound to themselves a strange example to follow for the advancing of their Discipline, Cha.1. Fol.129

Of their doctrine for making a reformation themselves and how the people must be thrust into that action, Cha.2. Fol.133

They would have the Nobility and the Inferiour Magistrates to set up their Discipline, and of their supplication with a hundred thousand hands, Cha.3. Fol.135

Presuming upon some unlawfull assistance, they use very violent words, Cha.4. Fol.138

Upon *Cartwrights* comming to Prison, some strange attempts were looked, Cha.5. Fol.141

One *Edmond Coppinger* took upon him to work *Cartwrights* &c. deliverance, he pretendeth an extraordinary calling, and acquainteth divers with it, one *Gibson* a Scot, *P. Wentworth, Cartwright, Wigginton, Chark, Travers, Egerton*, &c. Cha.6. Fol.143

How *Coppinger* and *Arthington* came acquainted with *Hacket*, of their conference with *Jo. Throg. Coppingers* letter to *Jo. Throg.* and his answer, Cha.7 Fol.152

Coppinger to *Hacket* of an appearance in the Star-chamber; his letter to *Udall*, why *Cartwright* &c. refused to conferre with him: *Cartwright* resolved some questions of *Coppingers*, Of eight Preachers that did fast and pray for *Coppingers* successe, Cha.8. Fol.156

Of *Hackets* first comming to *Wigginton*, of his gadding up and downe, and of the designement to have beene executed in the Star-chamber. Cha.9 Fol.159

A preparation towards the intended disloyalty, two of *Coppingers* Letters to *M. Charke* and to another: *Cartwrights* and *Wiggintons* commendation of *Penries* being then in London, Cha.10. Fol.161

Of the trayterous intendments which were towards the Court, Cha.11 Fol.166

That of long time some such attempts as *Hacket* made for Discipline, were of great likelyhood purposed, Cha.12. Fol.168

Briefe collections whereby it may summarily appeare, that certaine Ministers in London did know what *Coppinger* intended, Cha.13. Fol.171

The cunning dealing of certaine Ministers in London, how notwithstanding they wished *Coppingers* plot to go forward, yet they might be (if it were possible) without the compasse of law, Cha.14. Fol.173

If *Hackets* treasons had prevailed for the pretended Discipline, how they might have beene defended by the Disciplinary doctrine, Cha.15. Fol.176

FINIS.

Thou

Thou shalt not rayle upon the Judges, neither speake evill of Exod.22.28.
the Ruler of the people.

The Lord keepe me from laying my hand on him: For hee is 1.King.24.
the Lords annointed.

who can lay his hands upon the Lords annointed, and bee 1.King.26.
guiltlesse?

Speake not evill of the King: no, not in thy thought. Eccle.20.

Let every soule be subject to the higher powers, for there is no Paul to the
power but of God, and the powers that be, are ordained of God: Rom.13.
*Whosoever therefore resisteth the power, resisteth the ordinance
of God: and they that resist shal receive to themselves judgement.
Ye must be subject, not because of wrath onely, but also for conscience sake.*

We call upon the everlasting God for the health of our Empe- Tertul in A-
rors, alwayes beseeching Almighty God, to send every of them pologetico.
*long life, happy raigne, trusty servants, valiant Souldiers, faith-
full Councellors, orderly subjects, and the world quiet; and
whatsoever people or Prince can wish for.*

One night with a few firebrands, would yeeld us revenge Tertul. in A-
sufficient, if it were lawfull with us to requite evill with evill: pologet.
*But God forbid, that either they which take part with God, should
revenge themselves with humane fire, or be grieved to suffer
wherein they be tryed. If we would not practise secret revenge,
but professe open enmity, could we lacke number of men or force
of Armes? Are the* Moores, *thinke you, or the* Parthians, *or any
one Nation whatsoever, moe in number then we that are spread
over the whole world? We are not of you, and yet wee have filled
all the places and roomes which you have: Your Cities, Ilands,
Castles, Townes, Assemblies; your Tenths, Tribes, and Wardes;
yea the very Palace, Senate, and Judgment seats. For what*

warre

warre were, we not able and ready, though we were fewer in number then you, that go to our deathes so gladly, if it were not more lawfull in our religion to be slaine then to slay? Wee could without armes, neither rebelling, but onely dividing our selves from you, have done you spight enough with that separation: For if so great a multitude as wee are should have broken from you into some corner of the world, the losse of so many Citizens would have both shamed you and punished you. Beleeve me you would have bin affraid to see your selves alone; and amazed, as amongst the dead, to see silence and desolation every where; you would have had moe enemies then inhabitants, where now you have fewer enemies, by reason of the multitude of your Citizens that are almost all Christians.

<small>August. con. lit. Petil. lib. 2 c. p. 48.</small>
Saul had not innocencie, and yet hee had holinesse, not of life but of unction.

<small>Chrisost. de verb. Esa vidi Dominum.</small>
After the Priest had reproved the attempt, and the King would not yeeld, but offered Armes, shields, and spears, and used his power: then the Priest turning himselfe to God, I have done (saith he) my duty to warne him, I can go no further. For it is the Priests part onely to reprove, and freely to admonish (with words) not to assaile with arms, not to use targets, not to handle speares, not to bend bowes, nor to cast darts, but onely to reprove and freely to warne.

<small>Hie. lib. 2. adv. Jovinianum.</small>
Pateat quod noxium est, ut possit conteri cum patuerit.

THE

The first Booke of Disciplinarie Grounds and Practices.

Chap. I.

Of two sorts of men that especially disturbe the Church of England, and of the drifts of them both, by way of a Preface.

AS it is said of *Caiaphas*, when he told his companions the Pharisees and the rest, that it was expedient for them, that *one man should die for the people*, *Hoc à seipso non dixit, sed prophetavit, &c.* so in mine opinion it may well be said of the Pope, when he gave to the Kings and Queenes of England this Title, to be called *Defenders of the faith* : he spake not this of himselfe, but prophecied. For if any Christian King or Queene might ever be truly so termed, (as indeed it is a stile that containeth a great, and the most royall part of all their kingly offices,) surely of all the Princes that since that time have reigned, it is verified most properly in her most excellent Majesty: Whether you respect the Reformation of Religion, which her Highnesse hath made in this Church of England (according to the noble examples of *Moses, Iosua, David, Salomon, Iosaphat, Ezechias, Iosias, &c.*) or whether you respect, not only the relief, which strangers persecuted at home for the profession of the Gospell have here received: or her Majesties great and unspeakable charges, for the aiding and assisting of other Christian States, Princes, and

Countries:

Countries: that for their profession of the same right Religion, are mightily afflicted, by certain Gyants of the earth, the souldiers and members of that Antichrist of *Rome*.

So as in these and many other respects (which do concurre with them) I neither doubt that her Majesty (whom the Lord protect with his mighty hand long to reigne over us) shall be for ever renowned amongst the most famous Queenes, that ever lived in the world: or that the Church of England, so reformed by her Highnesse, is presently at this day the most Apostolike and flourishing Church, simply, that is in all Christendome. Howbeit let a Church be as richly planted as ever any was, before, or in the Apostles times: Let either *Moses* with his *Aaron*, or *David* with all his Councellors, governe both the Church and Common-wealth, as godly as ever any was governed: yet such is, and ever hath been, the malice and cunning of Satan: as that he wanteth not at any time, either will or means, to slander, to deprave, and to endanger the same. He hath his *Core*, *Dathan*, and *Abiram*, that if need be, dare presume to tell both *Moses* and *Aaron*, they take too much upon them. He is able to set the children of one father, the servants of one master, the subjects of one Prince, and the members of one Church, at dissention, at deadly hatred amongst themselves. As occasion serveth, he hath his *Shemeis* to curse King *David*, also his murmurers, complainers, mockers, makers of sects, such as *despise government*, which are presumptuous: men that stand in their lewd conceits: such as feare not to speake evill of those things they know not, and of them that are in dignity, that is, of Princes and great men, be they never so high in authority.

The experience which we have hereof at this day in the Church of England, is more than pregnant: partly through the divellish and traiterous practices of the Seminary

nary Priests and Jesuites: and partly by reason of the lewd and obstinate course, held by our pretended reformers, the Consistorian Puritanes: both of them labouring with all their might, by railing, libelling, and lying, to steale away the peoples hearts from their governours, to bring them to a dislike of the present state of our Church, and to draw them into parts-taking: the one sort, for the embracing of such directions, as should come unto them from *Rome*: the other for the establishing of that counterfeit and false Hierarchie, which they would obtrude upon us by the countenance and name of the Church of *Geneva*.

The which proceedings of both the sorts of disturbers, are so much the more dangerous, in that they deale so secretly, and have combined themselves, together with their Proselites, into such a league and confederacie; as get out what you can your selfe by meere chance (as they say) for the discovery of their actions, and attempts, you shall be sure that neither the one sort nor the other wil detect any thing. Nay matters being detected in some sort to their hands, they will utterly refuse to be examined, as law prescribeth: or if they take any oath, it is as good never a whit as never the better, they dally so exceedingly with it.

For under pretence of not accusing themselves, if they finde any thing to be come to light, which may any wayes touch them, they will utterly refuse for the most part to answer it, either upon oath or without oath: saying, that neither by the Lawes of God, nor man, they are bound so to answer. Under colour whereof they exempt themselves from the ordinary course held in justice, for criminall causes, throughout all the world: which is, that before witnesses be produced against any supposed offender, the party accused shall first answer to the accusation, yea, or nay, &c. as we use in England, and that in matters of life

B 2 and

and death (but in these without an oath) hee must first pleade guiltie or not guiltie.

And as they deale for themselves, so do they for their confederates, their favourers, relievers, abetters, and receivers: affirming it to be against the rules of charity, to bring their Christian brethren and friends into any danger, for doing of those things, which both the sorts of these seducers have drawn them into, and do themselves judge to be religious and just.

From these points all the Judges of the land, and divers Divines that have dealt with them, as yet cannot bring them: both the sorts are so setled in this seditious doctrine of *Rhemes*, which is as followeth, viz. *If thou be put to an oath to accuse Catholikes, for serving God as they ought to do, or to utter any innocent man, to Gods enemies and his, thou oughtest first to refuse such unlawfull oaths: but if thou have not constancie, and courage so to do, yet know thou that such oaths binde not at all in conscience and law of God, but may and must be broken under pain of damnation.*

Annotat. Rhemish upon the 23. of the Acts of the Apostles.

Now in these confederacies, what course should be taken for the preventing of such dangers, as may thereby ensue, I referre it to be throughly considered by those that have the government both of the Church and Common-weale committed unto them. But before they can be prevented they must be understood. Concerning the Seminarie Priests and Jesuites: their very comming into the land doth declare their traiterous intentions. What alleageance and love soever they pretend (upon their apprehension) to her Majesty and their countrey, it is very well knowne, they doe it but for the time, *rebus sic stantibus*, and that their comming hither, is to no other purpose, but to make a way for the Pope and the Spaniards; the sworne and mortall enemies, both to this state, and to all other

that

Book I.

that doe professe the right reformed religion of *Christ*.

But for the other sort of practitioners, their proceedings and designments, are not so well, as yet discovered. Their pretences do carie a greater shew of good meanings: and many (that are indeed truely zealous, little suspecting what hookes doe lie hid under such faire baits) are daily carried (as we see) headlong with them. In respect whereof, you are to be advertised, that as it is an easie matter by looking to the said Popish and Spanish practices, to know in generality, their Seminaries dealings here amongst us, be they in particularity never so secret: so are there certaine men in other countries, of the same humours with our pretended reformers, whose courses and proceedings, as well for the matters they desire, as for the manner of attaining of them, they propound to themselves, as the fittest patterns for them to follow: and namely the Ministers of *Geneva*, but more especially some of the Ministers of *Scotland*: as may hereby appeare.

As we have been an example, to the Churches of France *and* Scotland (saith M. Cartwright) *to follow us; so the Lord would have us also to profit, and be provoked by their example.* An other also in this sort. *Nobiles quidam præcipui hujus regni mecum egerunt, ut author essem regi meo de tollendis omninò Episcopatibus, ut exemplum postea posset manare in vicinam Angliam. Certaine of the chiefe Noble men of England (who I thinke now are gone,) dealt with me (by the instigation no doubt of some of our Ministers, Anno 1583.) to perswade the King of Scotland my master, to overthrow all the Bishopricks in his countrey, that his proceedings therein might be an example for England adjoyning.*

Upon a certaine repaire of ten thousand in armes to the King of *Scots*, at *Sterling*, Anno, 1585. whereupon the Bishopricks were indeed suppressed, *Knewstubbe* a Consistorian

A Letter of P. A.

Knewstubb

B 3

sistorian Minister of Suffolke, did write thus to *Field*: *I would be glad to heare somewhat of the estate of* Scotland : *it doth more trouble me then our owne : For I am conceiuing some hope upon the change of their former proceeding.*

It also appeareth that there is great and ordinary intelligence, betwixt their and our especiall presbyterie ministers, for the better, and more ready compassing of such devices and platformes, as are sought for, by our said ministers so busily amongst us. *The best of our Ministerie* (saith *James Gibson* a Minister of Scotland to a brother in England) *are most carefull of your estate, and had sent for that effect a Preacher of our Church this last summer* (1590.) *of purpose, to conferre with the best affected Ministers of your Church, to lay downe a plot, how our Church might best travell for your reliefe.* And againe: *The Lord knows what care we haue of your Church both in our publike and private prayers, &c. For as feeling members of one body, we reckon the affliction of your Church to be our owne.*

Gibson to Ed. Cop.

One *Davison* in like manner (an other minister of that countrey) taketh upon him to justifie the proceedings of our malecontent ministers here: (as it shall hereafter more plainly appeare) and for the better encouraging of them in their peevishnesse, he telleth them, *that the just defence of their holy cause of Discipline must not be left, which hath no lesse warrant to be continued perpetually within the Church, under this precept; Feed my sheepe: then hath the preaching of the word and ministration of the Sacraments.* He doth also publish it, so as the world might take notice of it: *that the good brethren of England, are of the same minde with them of Scotland, and that both their causes, are most neerely linked together.*

Davison against R. B.

Pag. 19.

Pag. 19.
Pag. 20.

Lastly there is almost nothing more ordinary, in all the Consistorian discourses and libels of our owne countreymen, whether they be printed here or in *Scotland*, then to
presse

presse us with the examples of *Geneva* and *Scotland*, and to inveigle the people of *England*, with (I know not what) great commendation of the proceedings and platforms of some of the Ministers in both those places.

Which points considered, and being required by those that might command me, that whereas certaine writings, and letters were come to my hands, concerning some courses taken by our said more friendly disturbers, than the Jesuites are, but yet very great disturbers; I should make the same in some sort known: I thought it my best way, for the discharging of my duty therein, first to lay down before you, the examples, patternes, and proceedings of those Ministers and Churches, which those our factious crew, propound to themselves to follow: and secondly (that I may not be enforced to passe by them, as one saith, D. B. was in his Sermon at *Pauls* Crosse) to make it most apparent unto you, how artificially and effectually, they have already by imitation expressed them. Whereby you shall perceive, that although by reason of their said combination and secretnesse used, many things be hid from those in authority, which they have done already, in the setting forward of their pretended discipline: yet there will fall out so much to be disclosed, as laying it to their patterns, you may easily discern (notwithstanding all their goodly pretences) what to judge of their proceedings; and whereat in truth they do aime.

[* Refor. no enemie. B. 2]

Chap. II.

Of the course held at Geneva, for reformation of religion, and of the doctrine which upon that occasion hath beene broached.

It seemeth, that when the Gospell began first to be preached by *Farellus*, *Viretus*, and others at *Geneva*,
they

they could have been well content with the government of the Bishop there, if he would willingly have rejected the Pope, and joyned with them for the reformation of Religion. This appeareth by M. *Calvins* words to Cardinall *Sadolete*. *Talem nobis Hierarchiam si exhibeant, in qua sic emineant Episcopi, ut Christo subesse non recusent, ut ab illo tanquam unico capite pendeant, & ad ipsum referantur: in qua, sic inter se fraternam societatem colant, ut non alio modo, quàm ejus veritate, sint colligati: tum verò nullo non anathemate dignos fatear, si qui erunt qui non eam reverenter summàque obedientia observent.* If they do bring unto us such an Hierarchie or Priestly government, wherein the Bishops shall so rule, as that they refuse not to submit themselves to Christ, that they also depend upon him, as their onely head, and can be content to referre themselves to him: in which Priestly government they do so keep brotherly society amongst themselves, that they be knit together by no other knot, than by the truth: then surely if there shall be any, that shall not submit themselves to that Hierarchie or Priestly government, reverently and with the greatest obedience that may be, I confesse there is no kinde of *Anathema*, or curse, or casting to the divell, whereof they are not worthy.

Thus farre then it must needs be thought, that the Bishop was offered by such as sought to reforme that Church: which offer he refusing (as I gesse) to accept of, they dealt (as it appeareth by the issue) with the inferiour magistrates and people, to make such a reformation themselves, as they required of them. Whereupon the Bishop being Lord of the City, and having aswell in his hands, the Soveraigne civill Jurisdiction over it, or (as M. *Calvin* speaketh) *Ius gladii & aliàs civilis jurisdictionis partes*, &c. as the Ecclesiasticall; they said, He was a thiefe and an usurper; and so of themselves, with such assistance as was procured, did thrust him from both those authorities. Even like (in my my opinion) as if a Christian Prince, being possessed within his dominions of the supreame Iurisdiction, as well in Ecclesiasticall as in civill causes, might upon the like occasion be served in the same manner: or, to prevent all exception, as if some Prince of some particular state or City in Germanie, taking upon him, together with his principality, the calling of a Preacher, Bishop, Superintendent or Ruler of many particular Churches, (as *George* the Prince *Anhoult* did) should in such a case (as the Bishop of *Geneva* was) be deprived of both.

<small>Ioach. Camerarius. Phil. Mela. Georg. Major de vita ejus.</small>

The meanes which was used, for such their abandoning of their Bishop, was this. When they perceived that the Bishop sought, by force to encounter their proceedings, and that (as *Sleydan* noteth) hee had excited the Duke of Savoy, to that end, to assist him: they joyned themselves into a more neere amity with *Berne*. So as the Duke and the Bishop comming together to besiege the City, they were both repulsed, *Bernatibus illis auxilium ferentibus*, The force of Berne *assisting the* Genevians. Since which time (as I suppose (it hath been a principle, with some of the chiefe Ministers of *Geneva*,) but contrary to the judgement of all other reformed Churches, for ought I know, which have not addicted themselves to follow *Geneva*) that *if Kinges and Princes refused to reform Religion, the inferior Magistrates or people, by direction of the ministery, might lawfully, & ought, if need required, even by force & arms, to reform it themselves.*

<small>Whittingham in his preface to Goodmans booke. Knox.</small>

Chap. III.
Of the proceeding of some Scottish Ministers: according to the Genevian rules of Reformation.

According to the reforming rule, mentioned in the end of the former Chapter, (to omit some other examples)

amples) certaine Ministers in *Scotland* with their adherents (being meere subjects) have taken upon them of later yeares, by a violent and forcible course to reforme Religion.

Knox in his hist. of the church of Scotland, pag 213.

In which course *M. Knox* a man trayned up in *Geneva*, in the time of *Mary* Queene of England, and very well instructed for such a worke, did shew himselfe to be a most especiall instrument, as it appeareth by a very strange letter, written by him from *Diepe*, Anno [a] 1557. Wherein hee sheweth, that his opinion and motion of that matter, was not grounded, only upon his owne conceite, but upon the grave counsells, and judgement of the most godly and learned, that then lived in *Europe*. (He meaneth the *Genevians*, *Calvin*, and the rest there.) Vpon this Letter and some other, to and from the said *Knox*, An [b] *oath of confederacie* was taken amongst his followers, in *Scotland*; and a testification was made of their intents by a kind of subscription.

[a] *Knox pag. 213. ibid.*

[b] *Knox p. 217*

[c] *Knox p. 218*

Immediately after, they prescribed also [c] *Orders for Reformation*, to be observed through all that whole Realme, Anno, 1558. And writ [d] a memorable letter to the *Religious houses*, in the name of the people, that they should either *remoove* thence by such a day, or else *they would then eject them by force*.

[d] *Knox p. 234*

[e] *Knox p. 256*

Shortly after (a *Parliament* being there holden by the *Queene Regent*) they [e] *protested* to the same, that except they had their desires, &c. they would proceed in their course: that neither *they nor any that joyned with them, should incurre therefore any danger in life, or lands, or other politicall paines: and that if any violence happened in pursuit of those matters, they should thanke themselves*. Afterward, (the *Queene Regent*, seing all the disorder, that was then, proceeded from such of the ministers) she [f] *summoned* them to have appeared at *Striveling*: which they refusing to doe, were thereupon by

[f] *Knox p. 258*

Book 1.   *Scottish Genevating for Reformation.*   11

by the *Queenes* commandement (as it is there tearmed)
put to the g *Horne*: and all men (under paine of rebellion)
were inhibited to *assist* them. But all this notwithstanding, g Knox p. 26.
their friends did sticke unto them. And presently after, up-
on a Sermon to that purpose, preached by *M. Knox*, in
Saint h *Iohnstowne*, for the overthrowing of Religious hou- h Holinshed
ses: they fell the same day to their worke: and within two p. 366.
dayes had quite destroyed and i rased in that towne, the Knox 262.
houses of the *Blacke fryars*, of the *Grey fryars*, and *Char-* i Knox p.263.
terhouse Monkes, downe to the ground. And so they
k proceeded, breaking downe images and altars, in *Fife*, k Thynne
Angus, *Mervis*, and other parts adjoyning. p. 366.
Buchanan.

This course being downe, and thereupon the sayd
Queene threatning to destroy *Saint Iohnstowne*, they l writt l Knox.p. 265
unto her, affirming that *except shee stayed from that crueltie,*
they should be compelled to take the sword of just defence, and *pro-*
tested, that without the Reformation, which they desired,
they would never be subject to any mortall man. Then they
m writ to all their brethren, to repaire unto them: like- m Knox p.268
wise *to the Nobilitie, upon paine of* n *Excommunication, to*
joyne with them: saying, that it was their duty to *bridle the* n Knox p. 272
fury and rage of wicked men, were it of Princes, or Emperours,
Knox pag.269.

Vpon these letters, divers o repaired to *Saint Iohnstowne* o Knox p.274
from sundry places: in so much as when *Lyon Herault in his*
coat armour, commanded all men, under paine of Treason, to re-
turne to their houses, by publike sound of Trumpet, in Glasco, *ne-*
ver a man obeyed that charg, but went forward to their associats.
They p writ in like manner to the Bishops and Clergie, p Knox p.275
that except they desisted from dealing against them, they
would *with all force and power, execute just vengeance and pu-*
nishment upon them: and that they would begin that same warre,
which God commmanded Israel, to execute, against the Cananites

C 2   This

22   *Scottish Genevating for reformation.*   **Booke 1.**

q Knox p. 276   This^q manner of proceeding, they termed to bee, *the resisting of the enemy.* After (upon conditions with the *Queene*) this great assembly at *Saint Iohnstowne*, departed thence. But before the severing of themselves, they entred into a
r Knox p. 283   ^r league by *Oath*, that if any one member of their congregation, should be troubled, they should all *concurre, assist, & convene againe together, for the defence of the same.*

Presently after (upon a new quarrel against the *Queenes* dealing) an other concourse was made of these reformers.
s Knox p. 289   at *Saint ^s Andrews*: where, by *M. Knox* perswasions in his Sermon, they made the like havock, that was before at *Saint Iohnstowne*, and did cast downe, spoyle, and destroy, both the houses of the Fryers, and the Abbeys in that towne. So dealt they also within a very short time, with
t Knox pag. 298. 299.   the Abby of *Scone*, the *Fryers* at *Strivelling*, at *Lithquo*, and Thynne, 367   at *Edenburgh*, the *Queene*^t being fled thence for feare. *They*
u Knox p. 300   *kept the field^x two moneths*, and tooke away to themselves
x Knox p. 306   the ^y *coyning Irons*, (being as the Queene alleaged, *a por-*
y Knox p. 308   *tion of the patrimonie of the Crowne.*) and ^z *justified the same.*
z Knox p. 308
a Knox p. 317   They ^a entred into a League, that though the *Queene sent for them, they would never come to her another time: without consent of their company.*

After, the ^b *Queene Regent* made a proclamation of her
b Knox p. 330   desire of peace, and that the state of the Realme, might at the last be quiet: but they ^c confuted it: and did animate
c Knox p. 333   those of their faction (with all their might) to be always ready, & to stand upon their guard. They gave the Queen
* Knox p. 361   the * *lie* divers times, and used her with most despitefull speeches. And at the length they came to that boldnes, as
d Knox p. 364   that they termed the *Queenes* part ^d *a faction*: and renouncing their obedience unto her, protested, that whosoever should take her part, *should be punished as Traitors, whensoever God should put the sword of Iustice, into their hands.*

Within

Booke I   *Scottish Genevating for reformation.*   13

Within a while ᵉafter, they confulted with their Minifters, efpecially *M. Wilcocke,* and *M. Knox,* for the depofing of the *Queene Regent,* from her government: who affuring the reft, that *it was lawfull for them fo to doe,* proceffe was made, fentence was given, and fhee was ᶠdeprived from all her regiment, by a formall act, which is fet downe in the fame ftorie, penned by *Knox,* and in fome part printed after in England.   e Knox p. 372
 f Knox p. 378

Not long after this: the *Queene Regent* dyeth. And then they had a *Parliament* by the confent of the French King, and their Queene his wife. In that ᵍ *Parliament,* held Anno,1560. they reformed Religion, and fet out a *Confeffion of the Chriftian faith:* but the faid *King* and ʰ *Queene denied, to confirm, or to ratifie the Actes thereof, when they were moved thereunto.* Which thing, (faid the confederates, upon intelligence given them) *we little regarded: or yet doe regard: for all that we did, was rather to fhew our dutifull obedience, then to begge of them any ftrength to our Religion.* And whereas it was objected, that it could not be a lawfull *Parliament,* where there was neither Scepter, Crowne, nor Sworde borne: they made light of it: ⁱ faying, that *thofe were rather but pompeous and glorious vaine ceremonies, then any fubftantial points, of neceffity required to a lawful Parliament.* I might proceed much further, in the ripping up of thefe and fuch like practices, for reformation of Religion. But becaufe fome peradventure, will labour to excufe thefe manner of proceedings, and to colour the fame, with fome pretence of zeale, and great defire they had, to bee delivered from Popifh Idolatry and Superftition: I have rather thought it convenient to let you underftand, how farre they are, from making any fuch pretences in their own behalfe, and with what new Divinity-pofitions. *M. Knox* and *M. Buchanan* have amplified the *Geneva* refolution (before mentioned)   g Knox p.468
 h Knox p.500
 i Knox p. 502

C 3

ned,) to the justification not only of all their said attempts and actions, but of many other of the like nature, which (since those times) have been there also practised.

Chap. IIII.
How the Genevian Doctrine, or principle for Reformation, hath beene amplified, by certaine pretended Reformers in Scotland.

k Knox p.216.
Knox appel. fol.28.

l Knox ap. 25.

m Knox to the Comminaltie f. 49.50

Reformation [k] of Religion, doth belong to more then the Clergie and the King.

Noble men [l] ought to reforme Religion, if the King will not.

Reformation [m] of Religion, belongeth to the Comminaltie.

n Ibid. fol. 47.

The Comminalty, [n] concurring with the Nobilitie, may compell the Bishops to cease from their tyranny.

o Ibid. fol. 55.

The [o] Comminaltie by their power, may bridle the cruell beasts (the Priests.)

p Ibid. fol. 55.

The [p] Comminalty, may lawfully require of their King, to have true Preachers: & if he be negligent, they justly may themselves provide them, maintaine them, defend them, against all that doe persecute them, and may detain the profits of the Church livings, from the other sort.

q Knox hist. pag. 343.

God hath [q] appointed the Nobilitie, to bridle the inordinate appetites of Princes, and in so doing, they cannot be accused, as resisters of authority.

r Knox appel. fol. 33.

It is their [r] dutie, to represse the rage and insolencie of Princes.

s Knox appel. f. 28, 30 &c.

The [s] Nobilitie and Comminalty, ought to reforme Religion, and in that case, may remove from honours, and may punish such, as God hath condemned, Deu.12. (he meaneth Idolaters, &c.) of what estate, condition, or honour soever.

t Knox appel. fol. 30.

The [t] punishment of such crimes, as touch the Majestie of God, doth not appertaine to Kings and chiefe rulers only, but also to the

Book I.   *Scottish Genevating for Reformation.*   15

the whole body of the people, and to every member of the same, as occasion, vocation, and abilitie shall serve, to revenge the injurie done against God.

The people [u] *are bound by oath to God, to revenge (to the utmost of their power) the injurie, done against his Majestie.*   u Knox appel. fol. 35.

The cruell murthering of the *Archbishopp of Saint Andrewes*, in his bed chamber, 1545. by three private gentlemen, because (as they told him,) he had beene, and so remained an obstinate enemie to the Gospell, is sought to be justified lately in print, to bee a godly act: and encouragement is given for others, in the like case to commit the like outrage.   History of the Church of Scotl. pa. 187

Princes, for[*] *iust causes may be deposed.*   * Knox histor. pag. 372.

It is not [a] *birthright onely, nor propinquity of bloud, that maketh a King, lawfully to raigne above a people, professing Christ Jesus.*   a knox to England and Scot, fol. 77.

If Princes [b] *be tyrants, against God and his truth, their subjects are freed from their oaths of obedience.*   b knox ibid. folio 78.

Populus rege [c] *est præstantior & melior: the people are better then the King, and of greater authority.*   c Buch. de iure regni page. 61.

Populo [d] *jus est, ut imperium cui velit deferat: the people have right, to bestow the Crowne at their pleasure.*   d ibid pa. 13.

Penes [e] *populum est, ut leges ferat: sunt reges veluti tabulariorum custodes. The making of lawes, doth belong to the people: and Kings are but as Masters of the Rolles.*   e ibid pag. 15.

The people, [f] *have the same power, over the King: that the King hath over any one man.*   f ibid pag. 58

It were [g] *good, that rewards were appointed by the people, for such as should kill tyrants: as commonly their is for those, qui lupos aut ursos occiderunt, aut catulos eorum deprehenderunt: that have killed either wolves or beares, or taken their whelpes.*   g ibid pag 40

The [h] *people may arraigne their Prince.*   h ibid pag. 62.

The

> ibid pag. 70.
k ibid pag. 70

The *Ministers may excommunicate him,*
He, *that* by *excommunication, is cast into hell: is not worthy to enjoy any life upon earth.*

And whereas there are sufficient, and sound objections, made, but such as have truely reprooved these dangerous assertions: Behold I pray you, their answers, worthy to be known and remembred, to the everlasting discredit of the authors, framers, and partakers with them.

CAHP. V.

The objections against the doctrine, reported of in the former Chapter, with the Consistorian answers unto them.

l Buc. de jure Regni. pag. 47.

Objection. Cvstome, is against such dealing with Princes.

Answere. *There is nothing more dangerous to bee followed (publica via) then custome.*

m Knox appe. fol. 16.

Ob. We must obey Kings, be they good or bad.
Ans. *It is blasphemie to say so.*

n Buch. de jure regni. pag. 53.

Ob. Jeremie commanded obedience to Nabuchodonazer.
Ans. *The example is but singular.*

o Ibid. pag. 57

Ob. God placeth tyrants sometimes for the punishment of his people.
Ans. *So doth he private men sometimes to kill them.*

p ibid. pag. 57

Ob. The Iewes dealt not so with their Kings.
Ans. *Their Kings were not first elected by the people; and therefore they might not: but ours have nothing but from the people.*

q ibid. pag. 57

Ob. Shew an example out of the Scriptures, that subjects may use their governours in this sort.
Ans. *The argument is not good: it cannot be shewed in the Scriptures, therefore it is unlawfull.* Possum apud multas nationes,

Book 1. *Scottish Genevating for Discipline.* 17

tiones, plurimas & saluberrimas recensere leges, quarum in sacris literis nullum est exemplum. *I can shew sundry good and wholesome laws in divers countries, of the which laws there is no example in the Scriptures.*

Ob. Saint *Paul* [r] doth command us to pray for Princes. 1 *Tim.* 2. [r Ibid. pag. 50.]

Ans. We may punish thieves, and yet we ought to pray for them.

Ob. Saint *Paul* [s] doth command us to be subject and obedient to Princes. *Tit* 3. [s Ibid.p.50.55.]

Ans. Paul writ this in the infancie of the Church. There were but few Christians then, and not many of them rich, or of abilitie, so as they were not ripe for such a purpose.

As if [t] *a man should write to such Christians as are under the Turk, in substance poore, in courage feeble, in strength unarmed, in number few, and generally subject to all kinde of injuries: would he not write as Paul did? So as the Apostle, did respect the men he writ unto: and his words are not to be extended, to the body or people of a Common-wealth, or whole Citie.* [t Ibid. pag. 56. Note this Divinity.]

For imagine (saith [u] he) *that Paul were now alive, where both the King and people do professe Christianitie, and that there were such Kings, as would have their becks to stand for laws: as cared neither for God nor man: as bestowed the Church revenues* scurris & balatronibus *upon jesters and rascals, and such as gibed at those that did embrace the more syncere Religion: what would he write of such to the Church? Surely except he would dissent from himself, he would say, that he accounted no such for Magistrates: he would forbid all men for speaking unto them, and from keeping them company. he would leave them to their subjects to be punished: neither would he blame them, if they accounted no longer such for their Kings, as by the law of God they could have no society withall.* And thus far the answerer. [u Ib. p. 56. 57.]

There are divers other objections against those reformers:

D

mers: which receive almost as desperate answers. But I will not at this time trouble you with them, especially if you will give me leave to advertise you, that this new Divinitie of dealing thus with Princes, is not only held by *Knox* and *Buchanan*, but generally (for ought I can learne) by most of the Consistorians of chiefe name beyond the Seas, who (being of the *Geneva* humour) do endeavour by most unjust and disloyall means, to subject to their forged presbyteries, the Scepters and Swords of Kings and Princes: as *Calvin, Beza, Hotoman, Vrsinus* (as he commeth out from *Newstadt*) *Vindiciæ contra tyrannos, Eusebius Philadelphus, &c.* For the further fruit of which Consistorian Divinitie, (besides that which is said by some of the Ministers of *Scotland*) I refer you to the consideration of such stirs, as have hapned of late yeares, in some other countries. And thus far concerning the justification, which is made of the Scottish reformation. Now I will lead you back againe where I left: viz. to certaine of the Ministers further proceedings there; upon these aforesaid maine grounds and principles.

Chap. VI.

The proceedings of certaine Scottish Ministers, according to the grounds mentioned in the two last chapters, for setting up of the consistorian Discipline, and of their urging of our English Disciplinaries, to follow their steps.

[Knox hist. pag. 502.] THe Parliament of Scotland before mentioned, Chap. 3. of An. 1560. being dissolved, there was then *a booke of Discipline*, or new Kingdome of Christ (by their severall presbyteries) drawne and compiled after the *Genevian* fashion, by *M. Knox* and others. Which book, upon the offering of it to their associates and favorites,

rites, to be allowed, received, and publikely practiced, was by them rejected, and termed to be in truth, but *a devout imagination*. Whereupon now riseth, an occasion of a new history, how (after they had obtained reformation of religion, as touching the true preaching of the Word, and administration of the Sacraments) they also dealt and prevailed in the end, for the establishing of their Discipline and Consistoriall government.

It * *appeareth*, that in the foresaid spoyles of Abbeyes, Frieries, and Cathedrall Churches, &c. every man almost did seek his private commodity. Which being espied before by the said Ministers, they misliked it: (as finding the prey taken out of their teeth:) but yet they were gone so farre belike, as that there was no remedy. They told them of it in their Sermons in some sort then, as it should appeare. Marry now, when they came to the end of their travaile, the hope of their glory, the erecting of their government, and their reigne over all, and do finde themselves crossed therein: blame them not, though they were not a little angry. Then * they gave it out against their owne favourers afore, *that some were licentious:* some had *greedily griped the possessions of the Church:* others *thought they would not lack their part of Christs coat, yea, and that before that ever he was hanged.*

* Knox hist. pag. 460.

* Knox hist. pag. 503.

Of a Noble man, that refused to subscribe to their Discipline, (as they call it) they writ thus. *He had a very evill woman to his wife: if the poore, the schooles, and the Ministerie of the Church, had their owne, his Kitchin would lacke two parts and more of that, which he unjustly now possesseth.* And generally to the like effect: *there were none within this Realme, more unmercifull to the poore Ministers, than were they, which had greatest rents of the Church. But in that we have perceived the old proverb to be true: nothing can suffice a wretch.* And

Ibidem.

D 2 againe,

againe, *the belly hath no eares.* They ʸ threatned the greatest men of the land, with Gods heavie punishments, if they should reject that Discipline, ascribing it to their *blind affection,* to their *respect of carnall friends,* to their *corrupt judgment,* and to their *former iniquities,* and *present ingratitude.* But ᵃ (notwithstanding, that some refused to subscribe to this booke, which made the Ministers so angry:) yet by sundry cunning devices, railings, threatnings, &c. many yeelded thereunto, and did promise, thereby *to set the same forward, to the uttermost of their powers.*

This subscription thus in sort obtained, they began to put the same in practice. They ᵇ appointed *to have their assemblies both particular and generall.* They ᶜ exercised jurisdictions, *and appointed one Saunderson to be carted for adultery:* but he was rescued. A great ᵈ uproare arising *in Edenburgh, about the making of a Robinhood, they of the Consistory did excommunicate the whole multitude.* The Bishops ᵉ seeking to encounter and represse them in their practices, they professed that they would not *suffer their pride and idolatry.* They ᶠ caused diverse places (as they termed them) of superstition, to be burnt: I think they meane some *Bishops* houses, as ᵍ *Palsay,* the *Bishop* also narrowly escaping them.

The *Bishops* having imbraced the Gospell, it was at first agreed even by the brethren, with the consent of the Regent, that *the Bishops estate should be* maintained and authorised. This endured for sundry yeares: but then there was no remedy, the calling it selfe of *Bishops* was at last become Antichristian, and down they must of necessity. Whereupon ʰ *they commanded the Bishops (by their owne authority) to leave their Offices and their Iurisdictions.*

They ⁱ decreed in their assemblies, that *Bishops should have no voices in Parliament:* and that done, they desired of the King, that such Commissioners (as they should send

---

y In the conclusion of their booke of Discipline.

a Knox hist. pag. 504.

b Declaration. B. 1. 2
c Knox hist. pag. 523.
d Ibid. p. 527.

e Ibid. pa. 531.

f Ibid. p. 534.

g Knox Iust. 534.

* Declaration. B. 2.

h Ibid. B. 2.

i Ibid. B. 2.

to the Parliament and Councell) might from thenceforth be authorized in the *Bishops* places, for the estate. They *also directed their Commissioners to the Kings Majesty*: commanding him and the Councell, *under paine of the censures of the Church* (meaning excommunication) *to appoint no Bishops in time to come, because they* (the brethren) *had concluded, that state to be unlawfull.*

Hereof, as it seemeth, they writ to *Geneva*, their new *Rome*, or *Metropolitane* City. From whence they were greatly animated, and earnestly perswaded, to continue in that course. *Beza* [k] the Consistorian *Patriarch*, assureth them that they had done well, and moveth them, *ne unquam illam pestem admittant, quamvis unitatis retinendæ specie blandiatur*: that they would never admit againe that plague, (meaning the calling of *Bishops*) although it might allure them, with colour of keeping unity.

[k] Epistola 79.

After they had discharged the *Bishops* (as it hath beene noted) they agreed amongst themselves, to have their [l] *Superintendents*. But that device continued not long: for in the end it was determined, that needs all Ministers of the Word, must be equall. And then (especially) their Presbyteries began to flourish. They tooke upon [m] them (with their adherents) *to usurpe the whole Ecclesiasticall Iurisdiction*. They *altered the lawes after their owne appetite*. They assembled [n] *the Kings subjects, and enjoyned Ecclesiasticall pains unto them*. They *made Decrees, and put the same in execution*. They *used* [o] *very traiterous, seditious, and contumelious words, in the pulpits, schools, and otherwise, to the disdaine and reproach of the King, and being called to answer the same, they utterly disclaimed the Kings authority: saying, he* [p] *was an incompetent Iudge, and that matters of the Pulpit ought to be exempted from the judgement and correction of Princes*. They [q] *prescribed lawes to the King and State*. They appointed [r] *Fasts throughout the*

[l] Declaration. B.3.

[m] Declaration. B.1.

[n] Act of Parliament.c.4.

[o] Ibid c.2.

[p] Decl.A.3.

[q] Decl.B.3.

[r] Decl.B.3.

the whole Realme, especially when some of their faction were to move any great enterprise.

With these manner of proceedings, the King there, and the State, finding great cause of just discontentment and danger: after diverse consultations and good deliberation, order was taken about the yeare, 1582. for the checking and redressing of them. His Majesty began to take upon him his lawfull authority, belonging to all Christian Princes, in causes Ecclesiasticall. Whereupon he caused the foresaid courses, held by the Ministers, to be examined and looked into. And they were found to be such, as that *some of them were removed from their charges, some were imprisoned, and some endited. Commandement was also given, that they should not proceed in the execution of their Ecclesiasticall censures, as they had done. A Proclamation was made in diverse of the chiefest places in the Realme, for discharging the Ministers of their foresaid conventions and assemblies, under paine, to be punished as Rebels.* They were published in that Proclamation, 'to be *unnaturall subjects, seditious persons, troublesome and unquiet spirits, members of Satan, enemies to the King, and the Common-wealth of their native countrey:* and were *charged to desist from preaching, in such sort as they did*, amongst other matters, against the authority in Church causes, against the calling of Bishops, and for the maintenance of their former proceedings.

But the issue of the Kings good intention to have reformed these disorders, was this: In August, 1582. his Highnesse being drawn unto a certaine Noblemans house to be feasted in Rutheuen: there *he was surprised and restrained*. Which attempt was qualified and termed (in a *Declaration* set out, 1582. to justifie the same) *to be onely a repaire of the Kings faithfull subjects, to his Highnesse presence, and to remain with him, for resisting of the present dangers appearing to*

Declaration 1582.

Act of Parliament, 1584. cap.7. Declaration 1582.

God

Gods true religion, &c. and for the removing from his Majesty the chiefe authors thereof.

After a time, the King delivered himselfe out of their hands, that so had restrained him: and by the advice of his three estates assembled in Councell, (notwithstanding the said qualification or pretence of repaire) the action in it selfe was judged and published in December, 1583. to be Crimen læsæ Majestatis, *the Offence of Treason*: and some were executed for it, others fled, and divers of the Ministers, that had been dealers in that matter, pretending they were persecuted, escaped into *England*. Act of Parl. 1584. cap. 7.

With this his Majesties course for Reformation, the Disciplinarian faction was greatly displeased: and did proceed in their Consistorian humour accordingly. In an assembly of Ministers and Elders (forsooth) at *Edenburgh*, shortly after, the State of the Realme was stoutly encountred. For although the King, with the advice of his estates, had resolved the said fact of surprising his Majesties person to be treasonable, *yet the brethren did not only authorize and avow the same, but also, esteeming their owne judgements, to be the soveraigne judgement of the Realme, did ordain all them to be excommunicated, that would not subscribe unto that their judgement.* Declar. 1585.

About the same time, or not long after, viz. in Aprill, 1583. there was another most treasonable conspiracie and rebellion attempted at Sterling, and intended to have been further executed and prosecuted against his Highnesse person: and all under pretence of Religion, and chiefly (in shew) for the Consistorian or Presbyteriall soveraigntie. Act of Parl. 1584. cap. 7.

With these and many more such undutifull insolencies the King and State there, being greatly mooved: a Parliament was called, and held in May, 1584. wherein order was taken, for a generall Reformation in causes Ecclesiasticall

clesiasticall, throughout the whole Church of *Scotland*.

^u Act of Parl. cap.2.
The Kings ^u lawfull authority in causes Ecclesiasticall, so often before impugned, was approved and confirmed; and it was made *treason*, for any man to refuse to answer before the King, though it were concerning any matter, which was Ecclesiasticall.

^x Ibid.cap. 10.
^y Ibid.cap. 3.
The third ^x estate of Parliament, (that is, *the Bishops*) *was restored to the ancient dignitie*: it was ^y made *treason*, for any man after that time to procure the *innovation or diminution* of the power and authority of any of the three estates.

^z Ibid.cap.4.
The foresaid ^z judgements, Senates, and Presbyteriall jurisdictions were discharged: and it was enacted in these words: *that after that time none should presume, or take upon them to convocate, convene, or assemble themselves together, for holding of Councels, conventions, or assemblies, to treat, consult, or determine in any matter of estate, civill or Ecclesiasticall, (excepting the ordinary judgements:) without the Kings especiall commandement.*

^a Ibid.cap.7.
It was ^a further then ordained, *that none of his Highnesse subjects, in time comming, should presume to take upon them by word or writing, to justifie the most treasonable attempt at Ruthven, or to keepe in Register or store, any books approving the same in any sort.*

^b Ibid.cap.3.
An Act ^b was also made, for the calling in of *Buchanans Chronicle*, and his book *de jure regni apud Scotos*.

^c Ibid.cap.8.
Lastly (saith the *Act* ^c *of Parliament* it selfe.) *Forasmuch as through the wicked, licentious, publike, and private speeches, and untrue calumnies of divers his Highnesse subjects, to the disdaine, contempt, and reproach of his Majestie, his Councell, and proceedings, stirring up his Highnesse subjects thereby, to misliking, sedition, unquietnesse, to cast off their due obedience to his Majestie. Therefore it is ordained, that none of his subjects*

shall

shall presume, or take upon them, privately or publikely, in Sermons, declamations, or familiar conferences, to utter any false, slanderous, or untrue speeches, to the disdaine, reproach, and contempt of his Majesty, his Councell, and proceedings, or to meddle in the affaires of his Highnesse, under paine, &c.

And thus you have seene some part of the practice of the *Geneva* resolution in *Scotland*, for their booke of *Discipline*, and reformation in Religion. But yet I must needs draw you on a little farther.

Presently, after that the said Parliament was ended, notwithstanding the Kings Majesty, had in the same [d] most royally and religiously confirmed with great sincerity the articles of true Religion, for preaching the Word, and administration of the Sacraments accordingly, and had likewise united to his Crowne, the supreme authority in all causes within his Realme, aswell Ecclesiasticall as Civill: yet (because their Presbyteriall Soveraignty was thereby abridged) diverse very spitefull, disloyall, and slanderous speeches were cast abroad, by them and their associates, against his Highnesse.

[d] Cap. 1. of that Parliament, &c.

For they [e] gave out, as though the King *had been declined to Popery, and had made Acts to derogate the free passage of the Gospell:* that he *endeavoured [f] to extinguish the light of the Gospell,* that there was *left nothing of the whole ancient forme of justice and policie in the spirituall state, but a naked shadow,* with many other the like reproachfull and calumnious reports, which they spread abroad in their own Countrey.

[e] Declar. A. 2.
[f] Thinnes addition to Holinshed pa. 446 D. A.

Diverse of [g] the chief Ministers of that faction likewise that were fled out of *Scotland* into *England*, for feare of punishment, in respect of many their great and hainous offences, pretended (as it hath beene noted) that they fled hither, because they were persecuted at home for their consciences, and could not be suffered to preach the Gospell.

[g] Archbishop of Saint Andrewes Letter, and of other Preachers.

E

pell: One [h] *Davison* (a Scottish Minister) so rayled against the King of Scots in the pulpit, at the parish Church of the old Iury in *London*, that upon complaint made thereof, by the Lord Ambassadour of *Scotland*, direction was given, to the Lord Bishop of *London*, for the silencing of all the Scottish Ministers in the Citie.

M. Hutchinsons Letter and as he is ready to be deposed.

And this disloyal and slanderous course was held, both in *Scotland* and *England*, so far as they [i] durst, from May, untill November following.

i Thinnes addition, page 116.

At what time, this stratagem here ensuing was wrought (as I am perswaded) by the Consistorians instigation. The King [k] of *Scotland*, being upon occasion of *a contract*, nere *Striveling* : heard of certaine enemies (*as hee then accounted them*) comming towards him. Wherupon his Majesty *raysing such power as hee could, convayed himselfe to* Striveling. Where before he looked for them, ten thousand men *presented themselves* in armes. *They pitched their Tents before the Towne the first of November*, and there made a Proclamation in their owne names, commanding all the Kings subjects to assist them. Many pretences [l] are alleaged of that their attempt. And these namely; That whereas there had been *Acts and Proclamations* a little before *published against the Ministery and Clergy, inhibiting their Presbyteries, assemblies and other exercises, priviledges, and immunities :* and that *the most learned and honest were compelled, for safety of their lives and consciences, to abandon their countrey, &c.* Now the *afflicted Church might be comforted, and all the sayd Acts lately made in prejudice of the same, might be solemnly cancelled, and for ever adnulled.* This Proclamation thus knowne, the King fortified the towne as he could: but to no purpose. For within two houres assault it was wonne. The King thereupon, was enforced to flye *unto the Castle.* The Conquerors of the towne, *placed their ensignes before the blocke-house of the Castle*

k ibid Thinn.

l The Proclamation is there also set downe.

Castle, and so ordred the matter, that there was no way for any in the Castle to escape their hands.

Whereupon (a parley being concluded) the King desired by his Commissioners three petitions: The first, *That his life, honour, and estate might be preserved.* The second, *That the lives of certain of his friends with him might not be touched.* The third, *That all things might be transacted peaceably.* The other side, by their Commissioners likewise desired other three petitions: The first, *That the King would allow of their intention, and subscribe their Proclamation, untill further order were established by the estates, &c. and that he would deliver unto them, all the strong holds in the Land.* The second *That the disquieters of the Common-wealth might be delivered unto them and abide their due tryall by Law.* The third, *That the old guard might be removed and another placed.*

Upon mutuall relation from the Commissioners on both sides, the parties that were assembled in armes, did yeeld unto the first and third of the Kings petitions: and the King granting to all theirs, as there was no remedie, committed himself into their hands, and had a new guard immediately appointed to attend him.

And thus the Presbyteries of *Scotland* by the Kings subscribing to the aforesaid Proclamation, recovered again a great part of their strength. But not al (as it seemeth) upon the sodaine: which was the occasion of a new stir. For presently after the said noble victorie, the *Scottish* ministers that were in England, (having all their former disloyalties upon composition remitted:) made their repaire without delay into *Scotland*: where finding not such readinesse as they expected, for a more authenticall repealing of the statutes made in the foresaid Parliament, 1584. they began (notwithstanding the Kings late goodnes towards them,) to exclaime in their Pulpits, with most proud and bitter

This appeareth by James Gibsons conference with the King, penned by himselfe, and delivered abroad in many copies

bitter Invectives against him.

One *Iames Gibson*, compared his Majestie publikely in his preachings, *unto Ieroboam*, termed *him a persecutor*, and *threatned him*, that if he tooke that course, he should be the *last of his race*.

Gibson hath penned this matter as Consistorianly, as Cataline himselfe could have done it.

And being called for such his disloyall speeches, before the King and Councell, the 21. of *December* 1585. he very boldly justified the same: saying to his Highnesse, *As long as you maintain these cursed Acts of 1584. the tyrannie of Bishops, &c. ye are a persecutor.* And again, *As Ieroboam for the leading of the people of Israel from the lawes of the house of Iudah, and from the true worshipping of God, to serve Idolatry, was rooted out, he and all his posterity: so should the King (if he continued in that cursed course, maintaining those wicked Acts against God) be rooted out, and conclude that race, &c.*

What else hath fallen out since that time, by reason of the raines, which now (as it hath beene noted) these zealous brethren have gotten to themselves, and how moderately and dutifully they doe proceed, in the practice of their Presbyteries, and Consistorian Kingdoms: the articles which the King not long since offered unto the ministers to have beene subscribed unto by them, doe sufficiently declare and make manifest. *Ex malis moribus nascuntur bonæ leges: Out of ill maners spring good and wholsome laws.*

The coppie of these articles, was delivered abroad by some of her Majesties privie Councell.

The chiefe and especiall points of the said articles are these: that *all Preachers there, should yeeld their obedience to the Kings Majesty: that they should not pretend any priviledge in their allegeance: that they should not meddle in matters of states: that they should not publikely revile his Majesty: that they should not draw the people from their due obedience to the King: and that when they are accused, upon their facts or speeches, or for refusing to do things, &c. they should not alledge the inspiration of the holy spirit, nor serve themselves with colour of conscience, but confesse*

Book I.   *Scottish Genevating for Discipline.*   29

fesse their offences as men, and to crave pardon as subjects, &c.

It is great pity, that so worthy a Christian King, should be driven to require such a subscription in his owne kingdome, especially of those men, that should be lights to the rest, and the chief examples of all dutifull obedience: It is more to be pitied, that (for ought I can learne) his Majestie cannot as yet obtaine so much at their hands. But most of all it is to be lamented, that no man can gesse (for ought I know) how far this Gangreene will spread it selfe.

At the first, they found but faults against the *Bishops*, but after they overthrew them. The *Anabaptists in Germany began with the Bishops and Clergy, but they ended with the civil Magistrate.* Consider of *Buchanans* dealing, whether he maketh not the like assault against Princes, that his companions did against *Bishops*, as in deriding their titles, misliking their pompe, and in glancing at their revenues. He termeth the honorable phrases of *Majestie*, *Highnesse*, and *Lordship*, solæcismos & barbarismos aulicos, *that is, unlawfull and corrupt kinds of speech, which are used in Court, and do proceed (as he saith) from flattery.* He gibeth [b] at the state which Princes take upon them, when they shew themselves to the people, comparing *them to childrens puppets, which are garishly attyred.*

After [c] also, he insinuateth that a good Prince *should appear & come abroad, only defended with his innocencie,* non superbo spiculatorum & μαχαιροφόρων cœtu, sericatisq; nebulonibus stipatus: *not with a proud company of guarders, and of pensioners, and of silken knaves.* He would have Kings to content themselvs with lesse *revenues and service, commending the Discipline of Laconia, where it was strange to have one man pul off an other mans sockes, at his going to bedde:* and likewise the example of *Pelagius*, that first discomfited the *Saracens* in *Spaine*: in that he had his house, *not built after the fashion*

[a] Epistle to the king of Scots befode his book de jure regni, &c.
[b] De jure regni pag. 17.
[c] Ibid. p. 34.

E 3   now

now a dayes, with many stately roomes of honor, but was contented *with one place for himself, his fire, his friends, and his cattel,* (after the Irish fashion.)

But to let passe these contempts and points of *Anabaptisme*: one thing more is likewise to be considered in these *Scottish* reforming ministers, which they have sucked from their *Mother City Geneva*. They cannot be content, to have raysed up sedition and troubles at home, to have slandered both farr and neer, the most G. d'y reformation of Religion, which their King had made there, and to erect (you have seene how) in place thereof a meere counterfeit plot of a new *Popish* tyranny, such a one as hath already quite overthrown the ancient estate of that Church, & wrought more mischiefe in that Country in thirty yeares, then the Pope of *Rome* had done before (as I thinke) in five hundred: but they presume also, much farther then becommeth them, to cast some of their contentious and disloyall seeds into *England*.

<small>* Melancton.</small>

Vulpecula* (cauda amissa) reliquis vulpibus callidè persuasit ut similiter & ipsæ caudas resecarent, ne sola turpis & deformis in suo genere videretur. The Fox (having lost her tayle) craftily persivaded the other Foxes, that they should likewise cut off their tailes, least she her selfe alone, should seeme the fowle and deformed beast of all that kinde. And hence it commeth (as I take it) that to bring the flourishing estate of our Church in *England* into the same misery, that theirs is brought into, they rayle, devise, and clap their hands, to set us here together by the eares.

<small>e Davison in the name of the rest, in a booke of his lately published. page 2. § pag. 29.</small>

Some of them say, that[e] *our Church is still under the bondage of an Antichristian government: that our Bishops are a hurtfull relique of Romish comfusion: that* ᶠ*they thrust with side and shoulder to make havocke of the Church, by a disguised persecution, and that they doe tyrannize above their brethren with*

violence

Book I.   *Scottish Genevating for Discipline.*   31

violence g *and cruelty.*   g pag. 28.

They use these words of her excellent Majestie. *Alacke good* h *Princesse, the true report of things commeth but seldome to her eares.* And do very grosly insinuate, nay indeed plainly affirm, that *there are in Court some crafty* i *miscreants, which doe abuse her Maiestie,* whom *they resemble to Ioab, Iesabell, Haman and Gehasi.*   h pag. 28.   i pag. 11.

They doo k *iustifie the proceedings of our disturbers here,* & *animating* l *them to goe forward,* as they have begun, doo tell them, *that both their causes* (vz. their own in *Scotland,* and of our factions in *England) are most neerely* m *linked together:* and *do* n *promise, that they will not cease to commend their troubled estate unto God, in their private and publike prayers.* They o compare our hindring in *England* of the pretended Discipline, unto *the hinderance, which Gods enemies made, unto the building of Ierusalem.* They seeke underhand p to steale away the hearts of her Majesties subjects, especially of those that have been, and still are seduced, by our Consistorian Schismatikes: by putting them in hope of *one Darius, that after a time shal give ful authority for the said building of Ierusalem.* Which manner of dealing, there is no *Darius* living, could take in good part, if the like practices were used by others amongst his people.

   k pag. 3.   l pag. 21.   m pag. 10.   n pag. 29.   o pag. 10.   p pag. 11.

GOD of his infinite mercy, grant unto her Majestie, a long, a prosperous, and a happy raigne over us: and so knit the hearts of all true English men, unto their Queene of Saba, their *Hester,* and their most royall *Elizabeth,* that without the expectation of any *Darius* whosoever, they may ever continue her most loyall, faithfull, and obedient subiects, rather wishing in their soules, that the world with her Majestie should end their dayes together, then once to take joy, by the least imagination of any future change. Amen.

                                         And.

And thus much of the manner and wayes used by certaine Scottish Ministers, for Reformation and Discipline. Which points or Consistorian proceedings, I have not touched (as God knoweth) with any minde or intent, to dishonour the state of that Countrey. Besides, much may well be said (I assure my selfe) in excuse of such of the laity; as joyned in the premisses. For I finde they were led with a very great zeal. They had been so long imprisoned in the darknesse of Popery, that when the Gospell appeared unto them, it so dazelled their eyes, as that for very gladnesse they considered not well, what they did, so they might enjoy it. Their goods, their lands, their wives and their children, nay their lives (in respect thereof) were not greatly deare unto them.

Moreover it is manifest, how long they were exercised with great feare and many perplexities, what entertainment and continuance the Gospell should finde amongst them. In which case every man may easily conjecture, how easie a matter it was for them, to be miscarried by their teachers and Preachers: perswading them, that by Gods commandement they were bound to undertake that course, and withall not omitting great threats of excommunication and damnation, if they refused so to do. They found their said Ministers Doctrine very good and sound, in the chiefe points of salvation: and who would then have suspected them in matters of lesse importance?

So as whatsoever was done amisse by them, as touching their proceedings mentioned, I do (wholly in a manner) ascribe it to their Ministers of the *Geneva* learning. Unto whom also it ought of right to be imputed, that I or any other, either have, or hereafter shall have, any occasion at all so much as once to make mention of the least thing, that might be any ways offensive to the meanest of that nation

Fo

For what had I, or any other private man in England, to doe with their matters, otherwise then to have prayed for them: had their said Ministers, but only taken upon them to have justified their said proceedings, by their owne Lawes, customes, and priviledges, and could have contented themselves to have gone no further? Marry now that the chiefest of them, for the excusing of themselvs, and that they might shew, whose schollers they are, have presumed to publish (and that in print) such strange and seditious doctrine, as doth tend to the like disturbance and indeed to the utter overthrow of the freest and most absolute Monarchies, that are or can be in Christendome, not omitting withall, to solicite and incourage our pretended reformers of England, to proceed as they have begun, in following their steps, contrary (I am sure) both to the word of God, and to all the lawes and customes of this Realme: I am in very good hope, that there is no man of any sound judgement, who will be offended with me, in that to disclose, and thereby to prevent such mischiefs, as might otherwise ensue with us, I have beene bold to lay downe (but yet out of their printed bookes) some of the proceedings of the said Ministers of *Scotland*, which at this time our owne Preachers in England, of the Disciplinarian consort, (as now it followeth to be shewed) do take upon them to imitate, and have already proceeded further in them, then some of their favourers will acknowledge or (I thinke) do as yet suspect.

<small>Buchanan. The historie of the Church of Scotland. Knox.</small>

The end of the first Booke.

F   THE

The second Book of Disciplinarie Grounds and Practices.

Chap. I.

The doctrine of certaine English Ministers, which they learned at Geneva, *and published of purpose to have procured the like course for reformation in England, to that which was in* Scotland.

As you have heard in the first Booke, how M. *Knox* being at *Geneva* in Q. *Maries* time, laboured and afterward proceeded to reforme Religion in *Scotland* by force and arms: so did sundry *English* men, that then lived there in like sort, according to the *Geneva* resolution in that point, endeavour as much as lay in them, to have kindled the like stirres at that time here in *England*. To which especiall end, they did write hither sundry letters and books, wholly of this argument: viz. *that the then Councellors; the Noblemen; inferiour Magistrates; and (rather then faile) the very people; were bound before God to overthrow the superstition and Idolatrie that was then in the Land, and to reforme Religion, whether the Queen would or no : yea though it were by putting her to death :* Out of two of these *English* bookes, I have collected these seditious and consistoriall propositions following.

All

Book 2.   *English Genevating for Reformation.*   35

All men, councellors, noble men, inferiour magistrates, and Goodman.
people are bound and charged, to see the lawes of God kept, and to page 73.
suppresse and resist Idolatry, by force. Ibid. pag. 74.
                                                  Ibid. pag. 77.

If the magistrates shall refuse to put massemongers and false Ibid. pag. 196.
*preachers to death, the people (in seeing it performed) do shew
that zeal of God, which was commended in* Phinees, *destroying
the adulterers, and in the* Israelites *against the* Benjamites.

To teach, that it was not lawfull in any case to resist the supe- Ibid. page 30.
*riour powers, but rather to submit our selves to punishment, is
a dangerous doctrine, taught by some, by the permission of God
for our sinnes.*

It is not sufficient for subjects, not to obey wicked commande- Ibid. page 63.
ments of their Princes, but to withstand them also, in doing the 43, 59, 72.
contrary, every man in his vocation and office.

Sheriffes, Iaylours, and other inferiour officers, ought not only Ibid. page 87,
not to cast the Saints of God in prison (having commandement 88, 89, 92.
*thereunto by the Prince) for feare of losing their offices: but to
withstand evill, to support them, and to deliver them, to the uttermost of their power.*

If we see a sheepe in danger to be devoured of a wolfe, we are Ibid. page 90.
*bound to deliver it : even so to our power we are bound to put to
our hands, to deliver the children of God, when we see them piti-
ously in danger, by Gods enemies.*

It is the office of Councellours, to bridle the affections of Ibid. page 34.
Princes and governours: Noblemen were first ordained to bridle page 35.
*Princes. Noblemen have their honour of the people, to revenge
the injuries of their Kings, and not for their lusty hawking,
nimble dicing and carding, singing and dauncing, open brag-* Obedience.
ging and swearing, false fleering and flattering, subtill pick- page 107.
ing and stealing, cruell polling and pilling, &c.

The authority, which Princes have, is given them from the Obedience.
people: Kings, Princes, and governours, have their authority of 25.
the people: and (upon occasion) the people may take it away again,

F 2

Ibid.pag. 105.	*as men may revoke their proxies and letters of Atturney.*
Goodman, page 190.	Subjects do promise obedience, that the Magistrate might help them: which if he do not, they are discharged of their obedience.
Ibid.pag. 119, 139.	If Magistrates without fear transgresse Gods laws themselves, and command others to do the like; then have they lost that honour and obedience, which otherwise their subjects did owe unto them: and ought no more to be taken for Magistrates, but be examined, accused, condemned, & punished as private transgressors.
Obedience, pag. 111.	Iudges ought by the Law of God, to summon Princes before them, for their crimes: and to proceed against them, as against all other offenders.
Goodman, 144,145. Obedience, 110.	Evill Princes ought (by the law of God) to be deposed, and inferiour Magistrates ought chiefly to do it. Examples allowed of Kings deposed. Edward 2. Richard 2. Christierne of Denmarke, &c.
Obedience, 99, 103. Goodman, pag.99. Obedience, pag.113. Ibid.pag.114. Ibid.pag.115.	It is lawfull to kill wicked kings and tyrants: and both by Gods law and mans law, Queen Mary ought to have been put to death, as being a tyrant, a monster, a cruell beast, &c. Examples. The subjects did kill the Queens highnesse Athalia: Jehu, killed the Queens majesty Jesabel: Elias, being no magistrate, killed the Queens majesties Chaplaines, Baals Priests. These examples are left for our instruction. Where this justice is not executed, the state is most corrupt.
Goodman, pag.185. Ibid.pag.180. Ibid.pag.184. Ibid.pag.185.	When Magistrates do cease to do their duties, (in thus deposing or killing of Princes) the people are as it were without officers: and then God giveth the sword into their hands, and he himselfe is become immediately their head: for to the multitude a portion of the sword of justice is committed: from the which no person, King, Queene, or Emperour (being an Idolater) is exempt: he must die the death. The people in the 25. of Numbers, did hang up certain of their heads and captains: which ought to be for ever a perpetuall example of their duety, in the like defection from God to hang up such rulers, as shall draw them from

from him. If neither the inferiour magistrates, nor the greatest part of people will do their offices: (in punishing, deposing, or killing of Princes) then the minister must excommunicate such a King: any minister may do it against the greatest Prince. God will send to the rest of the people, (which are willing to doe their duty, but are not able) some Moses *or* Othoniel. *If they know any* Jonathan, *they must go unto him to be their Captaine: and he ought not to refuse them. By the Word of God (in such a defection) a private man (having some speciall inward motion) may kill a Tyrant: as* Moses *did the Egyptian: as* Phinees *did the lecherous: and* Ahud *did king* Eglon: *or otherwise, a private man may do so, if he be commanded or permitted by the common-wealth.*

<small>Obedience, pag. 115. Obedience, pag. 116. Ibid. 118. Goodman, 199, 100, 101.</small>

<small>Obedience, pag. 110.</small>

And unto some objections that be made to the contrary, these answers are shaped.

Ob. Be subject to higher powers: the powers be ordained of God.

Ans. *Wicked Kings are Gods ordinance. Saint Paul speaketh of lawfull powers.*

Ob. Servants must be obedient to their Masters, though they be froward.

Ans. *Paul speaketh of bondmen, not of subjects obedience.*

Ob. Peter was commanded to put up his sword.

Ans. *He was a minister, and no magistrate.*

Ob. Christ could have called for twelve legions of Angels for his defence, if it had beene lawfull to have used force, for the setting up of the Gospell.

Ans. *Christs kingdome was not of this world: he tooke upon him no temporall sword: but that hindreth not those that have it.*

Ob. Ieremy was commanded to obey the king of Babel.

Ans. *The secret counsell of God was revealed to him to that effect. It is no generall rule.*

<small>Goodman, pag. 106.</small>
<small>Goodman, pag. 111.</small>
<small>Obedience, pag. 47. Goodman, 122.</small>
<small>Goodman, 119, 120.</small>
<small>Goodman, 125, 129.</small>

Ob.

38 *English Genevating for Reformation.* Book 2.

Goodman, 138, 139.]

Ob. David said, God forbid that I should touch the annointed of the Lord.

Ans. *It was in his owne private cause, and so unlawfull.*

Goodman. 102, 105.

Ob. Sir *Thomas Wyat* did, as you would have others to do, &c. but he had no good successe.

Ans. *The goodnesse of his cause is not to be measured by his successe.*

page 203.]

He was no traytour, his cause was Gods: and none, but Papists and traytours, can justly accuse him of treason.

The Councellors and all others, that would be accounted nobles (and tooke not his part) are in very deed traitours to God and his people, and to their countrey.

page 206.
page 207.

The authour of the book of obedience (he should have said of rebellion) endeth his treatise, with signification, that *the nobility of England,* (he speaketh of them that were in Queen *Maries* daies) *are not to be trusted either by their words, oaths, or handwritings, farther than a man doth see, and heare them, and scarcely so far.* And *Goodman* likewise, for his conclusion, is most earnest with all English subjects, that they would put his doctrine in practice, assuring them, that in so doing, if they be cast *in prison with* Joseph, *to wild beasts with* Daniel, *into the sea with* Jonas, *into the dungeon with* Jeremy, *into the fiery furnace with* Sidrach, Misach, *and* Abednago, *yet they shall be comforted: whereas if they will not: in seeking to save their lives, they shall lose them, they shall be cast out of the favour of God, their consciences shall be wounded with hell-like torments, they shall despaire and seeke to hang themselves with* Judas, *to murder themselves with* Francis Spira, *drown themselves with Iudge* Hales, *or else fall mad with Iustice* Morgan, *at* Geneva.

page 137.

page 218.
219.
220.
221.

In his preface to Goodmans booke.

This doctrine saith *Whittingham* (afterward unworthily *Deane of Durham*) was approved by the best learned in these parts, meaning Calvin, and the rest of the Genevians. The
English-

Englishmen of name, there at that time, besides *Goodman* and *Whittingham*, were (as I take it) *Anthony Gilby, Miles Coverdall, David Whitehead*, and sundry others. Who liking the said doctrine also exceedingly, were very earnest to have the *same printed, for the benefite* (as they said) *of their brethren in England*. *Whittingham* made a preface to *Goodmans* booke: wherein hee greatly commendeth this doctrine, and writeth thus, in the name (as it seemeth) of all his fellowes there. *We desire that you* (meaning all in *England* and elsewhere, that love to know the truth and follow it) *should be perswaded in this truth. Againe, here thou doest heare the* Eternall *speaking by his minister, &c. quickly give eare and obey, &c.* And again, *If thou wish for Christian liberty, come and see how it may easily be had, &c. From Geneva.*

Here it is very materiall further to be observed, that the rest of the learned men, that fled in *Queene Maries* time, as *Iohn Scorie: William Barlow: Richard Cox: Thomas Beacon: Iohn Bale: Iohn Parkhurst: Edmond Grindall: Edwine Sanders: Alexander Nowel: Robert Wisdome: Iohn Iewell:* and very many more, having no great affection to *Geneva*, bestowed themselves in *Germany*, especially at *Zuricke, Basil*, and *Franckford*. These men maintained the reformation of the Church of *England* in *K. Edwards* time: they used in their holy assemblies, the form of service, and order of ceremonies, which were then established: and they utterly misliked and condemned the foresaid propositions, as very seditious and rebellious, according to the judgement of all the reformed Churches, (for ought I can learne) both in *Germany* and els-where, besides *Geneva* and her off-spring.

Besides they of *Franckford*, (as it appeareth) notwithstanding their griefe, that they were constrained to leave their countrey, for their conscience: yet in the middest of all their afflictions, they retained such dutifull hearts unto to *Queene Mary*,) imitating therein the Apostles and Disciples of their Master) as that they could not endure to heare her so traduced into all hatred and obloquie, as shee was by the other sort. *Master Knox*, comming upon occasion from *Geneva* to *Franckford*, was by these grave men, accused of Treason, (as he himself confesseth) for matters that he had published in print, *against their Soveraigne and the Emperour*: and was faine thereupon, for the saving of his life, to flie thence secretly back againe to *Geneva*.

Knox hist. p. 185.

Lastly, by means of their disliking of the said propositions, and their further course held in the defence of the foresaid reformation in *England*, against the other mens counterfeit presbyteries: these learned men at *Franckford*, could have small reputation with them of *Geneva*. Thus one of that crew then, hath written since of them. *The English Church, which was assembled at Geneva, was separated from that superstitious and contentious company, that was at Franckford.* And againe, *They were more given unto unprofitable ceremonies, than to sincere Religion.*

Knox hist. p. 201.
Ibid. pag. 185.

These things I thought meet, for your advertisement, to set downe, that the propositions precedent might appeare unto you, not to have proceeded from any rash or light conceit in our *English* propounders, publishers, and maintainers of them: but that they doe containe their resolute judgement, agreeable to those points of the *Geneva* resolution, mentioned before out of *Knox* and *Buchanan*.

Whereby it is apparant, that if our said *English Genevians*, had found as ready assistance at that time in *England*, as *Knox* and his complices (about, or soone after the same time) did in *Scotland*, they would not have failed, to have put the said positions aswell in practice here with us, as some *Scottish* Ministers did in that countrey. Which great mischief, and disloyall outrage, as the state here, did then provi-

Book 2. *English Scottizing for Discipline by dotage.* 41

providently suppresse and withstand: So her Excellent Majesty, hath since prevented, by abolishing of the Romish Religion, and the restoring of the Gospell, which was the quarrell in those dayes pretended. So as our English Reformers, having hitherto had no cause for this point to imitate the foresaid proceedings in *Scotland*, it remaineth, that I shew unto you, how farre (as yet it is disclosed) and how directly they endeavour to follow the said practices of the *Scottish* Ministers, for the erecting up in *England* of the *Geneva* new Papacie.

Chap. II.

Our English Disciplinarians do imitate the Scottish in their desire of the Consistoriall government, saving that they are more bewitched with a kinde of dotage after it.

IN *Scotland*, notwithstanding that at the last the Ministers had obtained, in some sort, the allowance of the confession of their faith, containing the summe of that doctrine, which before they had so greatly desired: yet because they wanted the *Geneva* discipline, wherein consisted their very great joy, together with the hope of their future soveraignty, they were but a little satisfied with all the rest. And even so, it hath fallen out since in *England*, saving (for ought I can read) that the said *Scottish* Ministers were not then come unto so great a dotage after this Discipline, as here now is grown amongst us.

About some two or three and forty yeares agone, and after, in the beginning of her Majesties Reigne, the devisers themselves of this new platforme, were well content to accept of, and commend such Churches, as had abandoned Popery, though they had withall imbraced ano-

Harmonia confess. Cal Epist. &c.

G   ther

ther kinde of Discipline.

Then in disputation against the Papists and Anabaptists, there could be found in all *France* and *Geneva*, but two essentiall notes of the Church: viz. *the true preaching of the Word, and the right administration of the Sacraments.*

Bertram pa. 15. Mornay p. 37. Calvin.instit. Lib 4.cap. 1. sect. 9. Beza in colloquio Possiaceno. Convict. de statu Gall. passo. fol. 122. This appeareth by their Letters, Sermons, and by Gilbies most rayling Dialogue between a lame souldier of Barwick and an English Captaine.

Then upon *Goodmans, Whittinghams,* and *Gilbies* return, (with the rest of their associates) from *Geneva* into *England*: although it grieved them at the heart, that they might not beare as great a sway here in their severall consistories, as *Calvin* did at *Geneva*, and so not onely repined and grudged at her Majesties reformation of this Church, but laboured (as they might) to sow abroad in the land that seed, which hath brought forth a great part of all the disorders, troubles, and disobediences, that since have ensued. Yet notwithstanding, they meddle not much *in shew*, (for any thing I can heare of,) with matters of this Discipline, but rather busied themselves, about the apparell of ministers, ceremonies prescribed, and in picking of quarrels against the common Booke.

Confess. 5. & 7.

Marry since that, Maister *Beza* devised a way, how to bring in the *Geneva* Discipline, to be a third essentiall note of the Church: since, Maister *Cartwright* hath been at *Geneva*, and upon his returne did ingage his credit to justifie that platforme, to be a necessary forme of Government, prescribed by Christ for all times and places: since Maister *Travers* hath also been there, and did take upon him in his booke *de Disciplina Ecclesiastica,* to do the like: since, Maister *Cartwright* did likewise (at his second being beyond the seas,) send us word in his second booke, that Maister *Beza* accounted his said third note of the Church, (viz. the *Geneva* Discipline) *to be as necessary a note, as either the Word or Sacraments:* and since, Maister *Cartwright* and *Travers*, with the chiefest of their followers in *England*, have of

T.C. second reply. pa. 53.

later

later yeares (upon consideration of the premises, and further deliberation, in their conferences and meetings to that purpose) resolved and concluded generally, for the necessitie of the same Discipline, which before had beene onely delivered with us, as their private opinions : Since these times (I say) the friends and favourers of it, have from time to time, by certain degrees, so increased in their fond affections towards it; as that now they are in a manner overcome with the strength and violence of them, and doe brag in their bookes, that they will not sticke to die in the cause.

Master *Cartwright* (as I take it) had an especiall eye to this device when he saith, *that certaine of the things*, which he and his followers do stand upon, *are such, as if every haire of their heads, were a severall life, they ought to afford them all in defence of them*. Divers others besides, do offer *to adventure their lives for the justifying of it*, as *Vdall* and *Penry*, and nothing will content them without the *Geneva* discipline. For say they, *it is found * to be the only bond of peace, the bane of heresie, the punisher of sin and maintainer of righteousnes.*

It is, † perfect, and full of all goodnes for the peace, wealth and honour of Gods people, and is ordained for the joy and happinesse of all nations.

The want of the ᵖ *Eldership, is the cause of al evill. It is not* ᵈ *to bee hoped for, that any commonwealth will flourish without it. This Discipline* ᵉ *it is no small part of the Gospell: it is of the substance of it. It is the* ᶠ *right stuff and gold for building the Church of God. This would make the* ᵍ *Church a chast spouse, having a wonderfull brightnes as the morning, faire as the Moone, pure as the Sunne, and terrible like an army with banners. Without* ʰ *this Discipline, there can be no true Religion. This government* ⁱ *is the scepter whereby alone Christ Iesus ruleth among men. The Churches of God in* ᵏ *Denmarke, Saxony, Tigurin, &c. wanting this*

Epist. before the demonst.
Epist. before the sup.
* Practif of Prelates D. 2.
† Motion. pa. 46.
c T C. lib. 1. in the Epist.
d T C. lib. 1. pag. 3.
e T C. lib. 1. p. 6. and. 4t.
f Motion 84.
g Ibid. 84.
h Register. p. 68.
i Epi. before sup. A 2.
k Martin Iunior : Thef 14.

44　*English Scottizing for Discipline by dotage.*　Book 2.

l T.C. lib. 1. pag. 3.
m T.C. lib. 1 pag. 220.
n T.C. Table preface to the demonst.
o Motion to the Lords, pag. 22.
p Ibid. p. 49.

this government, are to be accounted maimed, and unperfect. The establishing [l] of the Presbyteries is the full placing of Christ in his kingdome. They that [m] reject this Discipline, refuse to have Christ reign over them: and deny [n] him in effect, to be their king or their [o] Lord. It is the blade [p] of a shaken sword, in the hand of the Cherubins, to keep the way of the tree of life.

Ridiculous men and bewitched. As though Christs soveraigntie, kingdome, and lordship were no where acknowledged, or to be found, but where halfe a dozen artizans, Shoomakers, Tinkers, and Tailors, with their Preacher and Reader, (eight or nine Cherubins forsooth) doe rule the whole parish. But I have noted unto you, out of these few places, (omitting many other) this their wonderfull dotage, to this end: that it may be considered whether it be likely, that our *English Consistorians* having over-run the Scottish ministers, or at the least overtaken them, in their opinions of the necessity of this Discipline, will be left behind them, in their practices according to the *Geneva* resolution, for the attaining of it, or no?

Chap. III.

Our pretended English reformers doe imitate or rather exceed the Scottish Ministers in rebelling and railing against all that doe encounter them.

WHen in *Scotland* they first had in minde to reforme religion, and after to erect their Discipline, (according to the *Geneva* resolution) they spent their wits and all their devices, by railing and slandering, to bring the Bishops and the rest of the Clergie, with the whole course of their governments into detestation and hatred with the people. They writ their owne pleasures of them, and to them: and

that

Book 2. *English Scottizing for Discipline by Railing.* 45

that in the name of the people. They stirred the Nobilitie by their writings against them: they had their supplications to their Parliaments: and to the *Queene Regent*; they had their appellations from their *Bishops*, their *exhortations* to the *Nobilitie*, to the *Estates* and *comminalty*, and many such practices they had to that purpose, yea, after their *Bishops* and *Clergie* had received the Gospell.

Knox hist. p. 234.
Ibid. p. 213. 214. 216.
Ibid p. 156.
Ibid. p. 304.

But in this course, our reformers in *England*, have not only imitated them, but (as ready Schollers, and apt for such mischiefe) have very farre exceeded both them, and (as I think) all others, that hitherto have dealt that way. They have renued over again, and applied to our Church governours, two or three of the most bitter Treatises, that ever were made against the *Popes, Cardinals, Popish Bishops, Monkes* and *Friers,* &c. in *King Henry* the eight his dayes. They have foure or five very divellish and infamous *Dialogues*: likewise their *complaints* and *petitions* to her Majesty and Parliament, in the name of the *comminaltie*, their *appellation*, their *exhortation*, and divers other most lewd and scurrilous Epistles and Letters.

Sathan Prince of hell, to the Pope, Cardinals, Bishops, &c.
Practise of Prelates.
1 *Gilbie.*
2 *I. B.*
3 *Vdals.*
4 *That which came from Throgmor.*

When they are called before any Magistrate, and dealt withall for their factious proceedings, they usually afterward doe take upon them to write and publish, under the name of a conference, what words and arguments have passed: which they performe with all reproch, disdaine, untruth and vanitie: and so do pester the Realme and their favourers closets, with infinite such shamelesse and slanderous discourses, as is most intolerable.

They have had five or six *supplications* to severall Parliaments, penned altogether according to *Knox* his stile and violent spirit, in many places word for word: besides *Martin*, and his two sonnes, their holy imitations of *Beza* his Passavantius, (that all things might proceed *Geneva*-like)

G 3 in

Martins Epi.
His Epitome.
Hay any wor.
Martin Iuni.
Martin Senior
Martin prote.

in their six bookes of *Consistorian* gravitie. And now, upon better care taken by her Majesty, that no such libels should be hereafter printed in *England*, (at the least without some danger to the parties, if it may be knowne) they have found such favour, as to procure their chiefe instrument and old servant *Walgrave*, to be the King of *Scots* Printer, from whence their wants in that behalf shall be fully supplyed.

Refor. to enemie.

For having obtained that place, (as he pretendeth in Print) they have published by hundreds, certaine spitefull and malicious bookes against her Majesties most honourable privie Councell. Also their *humble motion* to their LLs. with three or foure other very slanderous Treatises. And now it seemeth, for feare that any of all their said Libels and rayling Pamphlets, (that have bin written in her highnesse time) should perish, (being many of them but triobolar chartals: (they have taken upon them to make a *Register*: and to Print them altogether in *Scotland*, in two or three volumes: as it appeareth by a part of the said *Register*, all ready come from thence, and finished: which containeth in it three or foure and forty of the said Libels.

In all which courses taken, more then heathenish, this is their drift and especiall end, that having by their forged lies, their poysoned tongues, and their hypocriticall outcries, procured a generall mislike of her *Majesties* reformation, the present government of the *Church*, the chiefest defender thereof, the Lords that favour it, the *Archbishops* and *Bishops* that have authoritie in it, and the rest of the Clergy that do submit themselvs unto it: they might come at the last to attaine their purpose, and by fishing in our troubled waters (according to the *Geneva* resolution) set up and establish their glorious scepter and kingdome.

Out of these bookes, because some might otherwise charge

charge the premises herein with slander of the godly brethren, I have thought it very convenient to lay down before you, particularly, some most lewd and wicked speeches, in manner and order, as in ten of the next Chapters following, is specified.

Chap. IV.

The speeches of the said pretended reformers, concerning England: the state, the present reformation, and government of the Church.

ENgland [a] *with an impudent forehead, hath said: I will not come neare the holy one. And as for the building of his house, I will not so much as lift up a finger towards that worke, nay I will continue the desolations thereof.* [b] *England hateth them to this day, that faithfully do their office. Of* [c] *all the nations that have renounced that whore of* Rome, *there is none in the world so farre out of square, as England, in retaining the Popish Hierarchy.*

We in [d] *England are so farre off, from having a Church rightly reformed, that as yet we are scarce come to the outward face of the same. We* [e] *are never the better for her Majesties reformation, seeing the walls of* Sion *lie even with the ground,* (that is, seeing their discipline is not established.)

Your [f] *reformation (as it standeth) will be little better, than that of the Samaritans, who feared* Jehovah: *but worshipped their own Gods. Men* [g] *belike do think no more to be required at their hands, than the rasing of Babel: the divell as yet contenting himselfe with Bethel. Your* [h] *government is that, which giveth leave to a man to bee any thing, saving a sound Christian.*

Omnia cùm liceant, non licet esse bonum.

[a] Penries Epistle before the humble motion.

[b] Gilby p.77.
[c] Epistle before the demonst. B.3.

[d] 1.Adm.p.4.

[e] Supplic. to the Parliament, pag. 67.

[f] Supplic. 62.

[g] Supplic. 68.

[h] Preface to the demonst: A.4.

We

48 *English Scottizing for Discipline by Railing.* Book 2.

i 1.Adm. p.1.2.
k Epift. before the supplica.
l 1.Adm. p.25.

We [i] lack a right government of the Church. In [k] stead of the ordinance of God in the government of his Church, the merchandize of shamelesse Babylon is maintained. The [l] government now used by Archbishops, Bishops, &c. is both Antichristian and divellish. Rome is [m] come home to our gates. Antichrist [n] raigneth

m Gilbyes dial. 151.
n 1.Adm. p.33.
o Suppl. to the Parlia. 56.
p Hay any. p.a. 5,6,8,12.
q Martins Epistle. 33.
r Hay any. p.a. 13.

amongst us. The [o] established government of the Church, is trayterous against the majesty of Iesus Christ: it confirmeth the Popes supremacie, it is accursed. It is [p] an unlawfull, a false, a bastardly government. In the state of the Church there is nothing [q] but sores and blisters, yea the grief is even deadly at the heart: They [r] must needs be not only traytors to God and his word, but also enemies unto her Majesty, and the land, that defend the established government of the Church to be lawfull.

Chap. V.

Some of their undutifull and consistorian speeches concerning her Majesty, &c.

a Martins Epistle. 10, 53.
b Hay any. page 5.
c Ibid. p.g. 13, 15, 23.

THe [a] Bishops have long deceived, and seduced her Majesty and her people. Do [b] you think our Church government to be good and lawfull, because her Majesty and the State, who maintaine the reformed Religion, alloweth the same? why? the Lord doth not allow it. In effect: that [c] her Majesty and State, (in maintaining the established government, and rejecting theirs) do maime and deform the body of Christ, and so bid

d Register. p. 48.

God to battell against them. Ministers [d] ought not to obey the Prince, when he prescribeth ceremonies, and a fashion of apparell. By [e] the same authority, that the Queene commandeth

e Gilbyes preface to his dialogue of the souldier of Barwick.

the apparell, now appointed to the Ministers, she may command any piece of Poperie, so she name it policie. Achaz, of policie, brought such an altar into Ierusalem, as he did see at Damascus, where he had overcome the Idolaters and their Idols. But cursed

was

The II. Booke. English Scottizing for discipline by rayling. 49

was his policie, and so are all they that retaine any thing of their old Idolatrie, (he addeth for example, *the candlestickes upon the Queenes altar, kneeling at the communion, &c.*) *Of necessitie, all Christian magistrates are bound to receive this governement by Pastors, Doctors, Elders and Deacons, and to abolish all other Church governement. Either her Majestie knoweth not what they desire, being abused by the Bishops; or else shee is negligent of her dutie, and unthankefull to God.* [Martin junior. Thess. 22.] [Motion out of Scotland to the Lords pag. 41.]

Her Majestie, is cunningly resembled, to *Ieroboam, Ahab, Iehoram, Ahaz, Gedeon, Nadab, Saule, Iehu, Asa,* and *Iehosaphat* in those points, whereby they offended God, and shee is threatned by their examples, in that having begunne so well, she doth not proceede to set up Christs governement throughly. [Gilbie. 66. 68. 142. Motion p. 31. 32. 33.]

A question being asked (as the register reporteth) by the Bishop of London, Anno 1567, viz. *have we not a godly Prince? speake: is shee evill?* There are three answers made by three severall men. The first: *what a question is that? the fruites doe shew.* The second: *No; but the servants of God are persecuted under her.* The third: *Why? this question the Prophet answereth in the Psalmes: how can they have understanding that worke iniquitie, spoiling my people, and that extoll vanitie?* To this objection: that *it is Donatisme to challenge such authoritie over Princes,* (meaning the authority which the Eldership challengeth) answere is made: viz. *It is flatterie to suffer Princes to do what they list.* [Regist. p. 33. Wil. Whi. Tho. Rowlsd Ro. Hawkins] [Demonst. of Discipline pag 75.]

To this position: *That Princes should be excepted from Ecclesiasticall Discipline, and namely from excommunication,* they answere thus: *That excommunication should not be exercised against Princes, I utterly mislike:* To affirme that, *It is but a meere mockerie of the Lord, and to offer himselfe* (meaning the now L. Archbishop of Canterbury) *as a bawd to al maner of sinnes in Princes.* To insinuate, that others being subject [T.C. 2 part of his a reply pag 65] [Ibid. p. 92.]

H to

50. *The II. Booke. English Scottizing, for discipline by railing.*
to this correction, onely Princes should be exempted, (I feare) commeth from a worse cause then from simple error.

Chap. VI.

Some of their rayling speeches against the high court of Parliament; and all others generally that doe maintaine the present government of the Church of England.

m 2 Admonition pag. 3

For not admitting the platforme set downe in the first admonition, &c. Anno. 14. of her Majestie: and suffering the parties, that offered it, to be punished: Thus they write. The [m] *state sheweth it selfe not upright, alledge the Parliament what it will: all honest men shall finde lacke of equitie; all good consciences shall condemne that Court. It shall be easier for Sodom and Gomorrha, in the day of judgement, then for such a Court. There is no other thing to be looked for, then some speedy vengeance to light upon the whole land, provide as well as the politicke Machiavels of England thinke they can, though God doe his worst.*

n Sup. pa. 18.

o Sup pa. 15.

Likewise of the Parliament, the 29. of her Majestie (for their tollerating the Bishops, &c. in stead of their new government) it is said. That they shall be in danger of [n] *the terrible masse of Gods wrath, both in this life, and in the life to come: and that if they did not then abrogate (the government by Bishops,) well they might hope for the favor and intertainment of Moses (that is the curse of the law) but the favour and loving countenance of Jesus Christ, they should not see nor ever enjoy.*

Againe of the same Parliament, it is likewise affirmed: that (if the reformation desired, were not vaunced, they

could

The II. Booke. English Scottizing, for discipline by rayling. 51

should betray God, betray the truth, and betray the whole kingdome. They should declare themselves to be an assembly, wherein the Lords cause could not be heard; an assembly, wherein the felicity of miserable men could not be respected; an assembly, that wittingly called for the judgements of God upon the whole land; an assembly wherein truth, religion, and piety could beare no sway: There ¹ shall not be a man of their seed that shall prosper, be a Parliament-man, or beare rule in England any more.

 Furthermore, a prophecie is passed but from that spirit, I trust, that took upon him to be *spiritus mendax in ore prophetarum*, that if they prevailed not in the said Parliament according to their supplication, then ᶜ the Navy of the Spaniards should come againe, and fight against this land, and waste it with fire and sword: that God shall send a terror into the hearts of our valiantest and stoutest men: that one enemy shall chase a thousand of us: and that although we had smit the whole host, so as there remained none but wounded men amongst them, yet shall every man rise up in his tent, and over run this land.

 Lastly, this they write generally, of all that do withstand their desires: Those ᵗ kingdomes and states who defend any Church government, save this of Pastors, Doctors, Elders, and Deacons, are in danger of utter destruction. None ᵘ ever defended this Hierarchy of Bishops to be lawfull, but Papists, and such as were infected with Popish errors. No ˣ man can open his mouth (against Presbyteries) but with a shamelesse face, and seared conscience. The ʸ enemies hereof after the manner of the wicked, mentioned in Iob, do say unto the Almighty, depart from us, because we desire not the knowledge of thy ways: yea and in their practice they say, Who is the Almighty, that we should serve him?

 This ᵃ shalbe the portion of as many as (to the end) oppose themselves against the cause of reformation now laboured for: the heaven shall declare his wickednesse, and the earth shall rise

q Ibid. pag. 7

r Ibid. pa. 43.

s Of the Kings. 12
t Sup. pa. 75. 76.

t Martin junior. Thes. 18
u Ibid. Th 46

x Motion out of Scotland, pag 20.
y Epistle to the suppl. A. 3

a Epist to the sup: A. 4.

H 2   *up*

52. *English Scottizing for discipline by railing.* The II Booke.

up against him: the encrease of his house shall goe away: it shall flow away in the day of his wrath: his eyes shall see his destruction, and he shall drinke of the wrath of the Almighty. They [b] are no better to be thought of, then enemies to the Gospell of Christ, to her Majestie, and people: that seeke to keepe Christes holy Discipline from amongst us. This [c] is that cause, against which never man yet strived and prospered. All the Newgates and Oldgates, yea and all the Tiburnes in England, are too little for such rash, and presumptuous heads, that will not give God leave to rule: but will take the scepter out of his hands. I doe [d] feare that many of the forwardest enemies of reformation, are not the backwardest friends, that the king of Spaine hath in England at this day.

[marginal notes:]
Regist. of Scotland pag. 71.
[c] Epist. before the suppl. d Exhort to the B.B.B.
[d] Penry in his Refut. Scotl. bef. reformat. no enemy.

CHAP. VII.

Some of their Disciplinarian speeches concerning the Lords of her Majesties most honourable privy Councell.

[f] Our Councell may truely be said, to delight in the injury, and violent oppression of Gods Saints and Ministers: therefore the Lord will surely visit our Councell, with an heavy plague.

Our Councell [g] cannot possibly deale truely in matters of justice, betweene man and man; insomuch as they bend all their forces, to bereave Iesus Christ of his government. The which ungodly and wicked course as they have held on ever since the beginning of her Majesties raigne: so at this day they have taken great boldnesse, and growne more rebellious, against the Lord and his cause then ever they were. In so much as their honors in token of thankfulnesse to him that exalted them, dare now charge the cause of reformation, to be an enemie unto our state, and such as favor the same, to be unquiet and factious men

disturbers

[marginal notes:]
f Epist. from Scotl. before reformat. no enemie. A.3.
g Ibid. A.3. & 4

The II. Booke. English Scottizing for discipline by railing. 53.

disturbers of the common peace and quietnesse, and sowers of sedition among the subjects.

They doe [h] notably detect their impiety against God, and their enmitie to the kingdome of his Sonne Christ: they offer injury to her Majestie. If her Majestie give eare to such Counsellors, shee may have cause one day to lament. Assuredly those that are our enemies for the profession of the truth, (meaning the pretended Discipline) cannot bee her Majesties sure friends, whatsoever they pretend. [h] Ibid. A.4.

Sathan [i] worketh the defacing of the way of truth: & supporteth his owne kingdome, by instruments of no meane countenance. [i] Ibid. A.4.

Be they noble or [k] unnoble, Counsellors or inferior men: I am so farr from fearing their power, that the more I see them rage, the greater strength I have, to stand to the truth which they rave against. [k] Ibid. B 1.

I do warne [l] and admonish those Counsellors, with whom and against whom especially, I deale in this Treatise, to repent them of their great insolencie, whereby they have been puffed up with Senacherib, to magnifie and oppose themselves against the cause and people of the Lord of Hosts: as against the Religion and people of some of the Gods of the earth. Otherwise they are to feare least the Lord, having raised up many of them, out of meane places into the throne of justice, meaneth to shew his power and great name, by making them examples of his fearfull wrath, as he did Pharaoh, who wrought his owne overthrow. [l] Ibid. B.1.

If men will wonder, that [m] we being so contemptible in the sight of the world, dare yet be so bold, as to controll great states and mighty men; and to chalenge them of injustice, against the Sonne of God and his members; who will not sticke to brag with Pilate, that they have power to crucifie Christ, & to absolve him; they are to understand, that we know of no power, but from above: and therefore of no power, that is able to beare out injustice and wrong. The hils of the Robbers we grant to be high, [m] Ibid.B.2.

H 3 and

54. *English Scottizing for discipline by rayling.* The II Booke
and unassaileable in the sight of an eye of flesh: but we have
learned of the holy man, to account the habitation of the wicked
to be accursed, even when he seemeth to be best rooted: for we
know that the steps of his strength shall be restrained, and that
his counsaile shall cast him downe.

CHAP. VIII.

Some of their rayling speeches against the Magistracy in England, the Iudges, Lawyers, and Lawes, both Civill and Ecclesiasticall.

_{a Epist. from Scotl. before reformat. no enemy A. 3.}
_{a Ibid. A. 3.}

THE [a] *Magistracy and Ministery have walked hand in hand, in the contempt of true Religion: and unto both the Word of the Lord is made a reproach.*

Amongst [a] *those who deale in the cause of justice, there are found wicked persons, even wicked Lawyers and Iudges, (who seeme to know of no other God, but their owne gaine,) that lay wait for the bloud of Gods Saints, as he that setteth snares; and marke whether they can heare of any, that go farther in the cause of God, than the corruption of our state doth permit. And if they finde any such, they know how to wrest against them a clause of some statute, contrary not onely to the meaning thereof, but even contrary unto all justice and equity, yea common reason it selfe, and the very grounds of all good Lawes and Statutes. So that it is now growne, and hath been of a long time a common practice of these godlesse men, to make of the Statutes, ordained for the maintenance of Religion and common quietnesse, a pit, whereinto catch the peaceable of the land.*

_{b Ibid. A. 3.}

The common [b] *indictements of the Lords true and faithfull Ministers, for matters of trifles, as the omission of the Surplice, churching of women, crosse in Baptisme, &c. doth manifestly witnesse the iniquity of these Atheists.*

The

The II. Booke English Scottizing, for discipline by rayling. 55.

The [q] lawes, that maintaine the Archbishops and Bishops are no more to bee accounted of, then the lawes maintaining the Stewes.

The [r] humane lawes, that maintaine them, are wicked and ungodly.

The lawes [s] are made their common sanctuarie, to defend all our wickednesse.

Impietie is [t] suffered to beare sway against the Majestie of God: and that by law and authority.

Such lawes [u] are retained in force, as justle and overthrow the royall prerogative of the sonne of God.

As [x] great indignitie is offered unto Iesus Christ, in committing his Church unto the government of the common law, as can be, by meane hirelings unto a king: in committing his beloved spouse unto the direction of the mistresse of the Stewes, and enforcing her to live after the lawes of a brothel-house.

[q] Martin Iunior. Thes. 34.
[r] ibid. Thes. 38.
[s] Fenner against Bridges. p. 5.
[t] Sup. pa. 59.
[u] Sup. pa. 24.
[x] Epistle before the demonst. B. 4.

Chap. IX.
Some of their consistoriall sayings, as touching our Religion, Communion booke, Sacraments and Ceremonies.

WE [a] strive for true religion. As [b] our lackes are, there can be no right religion. [c] Many religions are mixed together, of Christ and Antichrist, of God and the devill. [d] *Christs Religion is fondly patched with the Popes; joyning fire and water, heaven and hell together.* The [e] truth (in a manner) doth but peepe out from behinde the screene.

Their [f] prescript forme of service is full of corruption. In all the order of their service, there is no edification, but confusion. The [h] Communion booke is an unperfect booke, culled and picked out of that popish dunghill, the portuise and masse-booke:

and

[a] 1. Adm. 32
[b] Ibid. pag. 2
[c] Gilby. p. 29
[d] ibid. pag. 90
[e] 2 Adm. p. 6.
[f] 1. Adm. p. 17
[g] ibid. pag. 24
[h] ibid. pag. 16

56 *English Scottizing, for discipline by rayling.* The II. Booke. and many of the contents therein be such, as are against the word of God. And [i] *Martin senior* calleth it our *sterve-us booke.*

[i Martin senior, C. 2.]

The [k] *Sacraments are wickedly mangled and prophaned.* They [l] *eate not the Lords supper, but play a pageant of their own, to blinde the people: and keepe them still in superstition: to make the silly soules beleeve that they have an English masse: and so put no difference betwixt truth and falsehood, betwixt Christ and Antichrist, betwixt God and the devill.* [m] *The publike baptisme is full of childish and superstitious toyes.*

[k 2. Admon. pag. 42.]
[l Gilby pag. 2]
[m 1 Admon. pag. 21.]

And of our orders, garments, and ceremonies. They are [n] *carnall, beggerly, Antichristian pompes, rights, lawes, and traditions: popish fooleries, Romish reliques, and rags of Antichrist, dregs and remnants of transformed Poperie : Pharisaicall outward faces and vizards: remnants of Romish Antichrist of superstition, and Idolatrie: Knowne liveries of Antichrist: accursed leaven of the blasphemous Popish Priesthoode, cursed patches of Poperie and Idolatrie, they are worse then lowsie: for they are sibbe to the sarke of* Hercules, *that made him teare his owne bowels asunder.*

[n Gilby. p. 40]
[pag. 41.]
[pag. 1.]
[pag. 5.]
[pag. 12]
[pag. 14.]
[pag. 91]
[pag 96]
[pag 95.]
[pag. 150.]

Chap. X.
How they charge the present government with persecution.

[H]Ere is [o] *a persecution of poore Christians, and the professors of the Gospell suffered, not far unlike to the sixe articles.* Gods [p] *cause is troden under foote, and the benefit of his Church is little regarded.*

[o 2 Admon. pag. 59.]
[p ibid.]

[q] *Poore men have beene miserably handled, with revilings, deprivations, imprisonments, banishments, and such like extremities.* Godly [r] *Ministers have beene brought before the barres of justice: they have been arraigned amongst fellons and theeves: they have beenimprisoned to the uttermost and defaced: they are reproched*

[q 1 Adm. p. 2]
[r Practise of Prelates, D. 8]

Book 2.   *English Scottizing for Discipline by rayling.*   57

reproached, shaken up, threatned; many are deprived: they are examined by an inquisition, much like that of Spaine. O lamentable case! O hainous impiety!

Shall they be thus marked with the black cole of reproach and villanie? O inhumane, and more than barbarous impiety!   f Ibid.B.1.

Besides *whorish impudency, halter, axe, bands, scourging, and racking, our Bishops have nothing to defend themselves withall.*   t Mart. protest. 13.

The ᵘ *Clink, Gate-house, White-Lion, and the Fleet, are their onely arguments.*   u Vdall dialogue. F.1.

If ᵃ *Isay, Jeremie, Ezechiel, Osee, Micheas, and Zachary were alive, they would be carried to the Marshall-sea, the White-lyon, the Kings-bench, the Gate-house, and other prisons, yea to New-gate.*   a Exhort. to BB.A.1.

In ᵇ effect, as *Cain persecuted* Abel: Esau, Jacob: the Patriarchs, their brother Joseph: the Iewes, Moses the Priests Ieremie, Osea, Amazia and Christ: *even so in these dayes, the Preachers are slandered and persecuted by such, as would seeme pillars of true religion. If this persecution* ᶜ *be not provided for, it is the case of many a thousand in* England, *great troubles will come of it.*   b 1.Admon. pag.1. & 2.   c pag.59.

The ᵈ *land is sore troubled: there is no place nor being for a faithfull Minister of the Word. Our bloud crieth for vengeance against the Bishops.*   d Dialogue that came from Throg.D.2.

I ᵉ *am made like to our Saviour Christ, who hath troden this path, in that (as he saith) he is troubled not for evill, but for good. It* ᶠ *fares with us as with prisoners in Popery: God send us their comfort. Ministers* ᵍ *are in worse sort suppressed now, than they were by the Papists in Queene Maries time. This crosse* ʰ *is common, not onely with him, but with all that will live godly in Christ. The cause is holy, and his sufferings acceptable. I* ⁱ *perceive the Lion roareth, but cannot bite, farther than the Lord shall permit.*   e Martin. protest.pag.5.   f Snape to his father,1500.   g Wight before he was imprisoned to a friend.   h Lord in his papers.   i Pen of [..] imprison[..]

I   Chap.

Chap. XI.

Some of their Consistorian speeches of the Clergie of England, assembled, as occasion hath required, in the Convocation house.

l Sup.p.47.
pag. 48.
pag. 49.
pag. 53.

THey [l] are wolves. It is a Synagogue. Their onely endeavour is, how to prevent Christ, from bearing rule in the Church, by his owne lawes. They are knowne to be enemies unto all sincerity. The whole Convocation house are (in judgement) contrary to our Saviour Christ, they are intolerable oppugners of Gods glory: and utter enemies unto the liberties of his Church. As long as that house standeth, (as at this day it doth) there can be no hope at all, that either Gods heavenly truth

pag.55.

should have free passage, or the Church her liberty, in this kingdome. They have seduced and deceived the civill state, and people, in bearing them in hand, that all is well in the Church.

m Mart. Epist.

They are termed (by one of the [m] Captaines of this crue) right puissant, poysoned, persecuting, and terrible Priests: Clergie maisters of the confocation house: the holy league of subscription: the crue of monstrous and ungodly wretches, that mingle heaven and earth together: horned maisters of the conspiration house: an Antichristian swinish rabble: enemies of the Gospell: most covetous, wretched and Popish Priests, the Con-

n Dialogue tha. came from Throgmort. D.4.

vocation house of Divels, Belzabub [n] of Canterbury, the chief of the Divels.

Chap. XII.

Some of their presbyteriall speeches of the Bishops of England, professing the Gospell.

o Hay any.p. 15.14,&c.

THe [o] Bishops are the greatest and most pestilent enemies that now our state hath, and are like to be the ruine of her

Majesty

Book 2.   *English Scottizing for Discipline by railing.*   59

Majestie, and the whole state : Archbishops and Bishops are un-   pag. 10.
lawfull, unnaturall, false, and bastardie governours of the
Church, and the ordinances of the Divell : pettie Popes : pettie   pag. 11.
Antichrists : like incarnate Divels : they are Bishops of the Divell : Bishops [p] are cogging and cosening knaves. They will lie   Ibid. 28.
like dogs.   Our [q] Bishops are proud, popish, presumptuous, pro-   p Martins Epist. 37.
phane, paltrie, pestilent, pernicious prelates, and usurpers : Im-   q Epist. pag 6.
pudent, shamelesse, and wainscot faced Bishops, like beasts. They
are in a premunire. They ought not to be maintained by the au-   pag 33.
thority of the civill Magistrate, in any common-wealth. They   pag. 31.
are in respect of their places, enemies of God. The (worst Pu-   pag. 4.
ritane is an honester man, then the best Lord Bishop in Christen-   r V. als Dialogue c. 1.
dome.   s Martins
   Their [s] crueltie is without measure. They are butchers and   protest. 27.
horsleeches : it is the portion of their inheritance. Their blood-   t Martins protest. pag. 4.
thirstie attempts. These dragons. Their tyrannie and blood-thir-   pag. 8.
sty proceedings are inexcusable. In effect, that they conspire to pull   pag. 12.
the Crown from her Majesties head.   pag. 21.
      pag. 26.
   Bishops [u] callings are meere antichristian. The [x] Bishops are
robbers, Wolves, simoniacks, persecutors, sowers of sedition and   u Vdals dialogue D. 1.
discontentednesse betweene her Majesties subjects. They have in-
curred the statute of premunire : they are (ipso facto) deprivable.   x Martin sen. B. 4. c. 1
Though they be in the Church ; yet they are none of the Church.
The true Church of God ought to have no more to do with them,
and the Synagogue, (namely their Antichristian Courts) then
with the Synagogue of Sathan. Be [a] packing Bishops : you strive   a Epist. to the
in vaine, you are laid open already. Friers and Monkes were not   epitome.
so bad.

   Of [b] all the Bishops that ever were in the See of the Archbi-   b The Dialog
shop of Canterbury, there was never any did so much hurt to the   that came from
Church of God as he hath done.   No Bishop that ever had such   Throgmort.
an aspiring and Ambitious minde as hee, no not Cardinall Wol-   D. 3.
cey. None so proud as he : No not Stephen Gardiner of Winche-

I 2   ster

60 *English Scottizing for Discipline by railing.* Book 2.

c Ibid.c.4. ſter. None ſo tyrannicall as he: no not Bonner. He ſits c upon his cogging ſtoole, which may truly be called, the chaire of peſtilence. His mouth is full of curſing againſt God and his Saints.

Mart.ſen.c.2. His feet are ſwift to ſhed blood: there is none of Gods children, but had as lieve ſee a Serpent, as meet him. It grieveth them

d Mart.ſen. to ſee ſo wicked an enemie of God and his Church. Belzebub d of Canterbury. The Canterbury Caiaphas: Eſau: a monſtrous Antichriſtian Pope: a moſt bloodie oppreſſour of Gods Saints:

e Epiſtle out of Scotl. before reforma. no enemie. a very Antichriſtian beaſt a moſt vile and curſed tyrant. In e reſpect of his Antichriſtian prelacie over Gods Church, and for the notable hatred, which hee hath ever bewrayed towards the Lord and his truth, I thinke him one of the diſhonourableſt creatures under heaven.

f praƈice of Prelates c. 6. And again f of the Biſhops, but eſpecially of the Lord Archbiſhop. In his behaviour, wrath, anger, reproach, and diſdaine (as in a wood, ſo many Lions, Beares, Tigers, and cruell beaſts) were ſeene to range, and in this more ſalvage, that whereas they by time and uſage may be tamed and appeaſed, this

g Supp.37. man never. It g would be knowne, whether they have ſome ſecret meaning, if opportunitie would ſerve to aſpire unto the Crowne.

Chap. XIII.

Some of their uncharitable words againſt all the Clergie in England, generally that miſlike their deſignements.

h 1. Adm p.2. i Ibid. pag.4. k Mr. Iu. C.2 WE lack in England a right miniſtery of God. The h Miniſters are neither prooved, elected, called, nor ordeined according to Gods word. I B. is to be k inveſted into the place of a naturall foole, after a ſolemne manner, according to the book of ordaining Biſhops and Prieſts.

The

Book 2.   *English Scottizing for Discipline by railing.*   61.

The [l] *Clergie is indicted, as the followers of Antichrist, and that their Ministerie is from the Pope. Little* [m] *or nothing is required of our English Priests; but to say the Catechisme, and to weare a cap, coap and tippet: Antichrists rags shall make him a Priest, be he never such a dolt or villaine.*

The [n] *most part of Our Ministers, are either Popish Priests, or Monkes, or Fryers, or ale-house haunters, or boyes and lads, drunkards and dolts: that will weare a fooles hood, for living sake: They are Hogs, Dogs, Wolves, Foxes, Simoniakes, Vsurers: procters of Antichrists inventions: Popish chapmen, halting Neutrals. They seeke nothing, but like greedy Dogs, how to fill their paunches.*

Our supposed Ministers are a multitude of desperate and forelorne Atheists, a cursed, uncircumcised, and murthering generation, you shall finde amongst this crue nothing else, but a troope of bloodie soule murtherers, and sacrilegious Church-robbers. Bene quod malitia non habet tantas vires, quantos conatus.

l Exhort. to BB: B. 1.
m Gilby. p. 50.
Ibid. pag. 3.

n Gil. p. 111.

pag. 53.
pag. 32.
pag. 89.
pag. 112.

Epist. from Scotl. before reformat. no. enemy A. 3.
Hier. lib. 2. con. Ruffin.

Chap. XIV.

Their especiall drift in their said railing speeches, as outragiously published, as if they were meere Jesuites, and peradventure to as dangerous a purpose.

BY the former so wicked and slaunderous speeches, contained in the ten last Chapters, you see how the brotherhood endevoureth with the multitude (as I said) not only the disgrace of our Church and Clergiemen, but likewise how bold they are with her most excellent Majestie: the high Court of Parliament, the Lords of her privie Councell: the Judges, Lawyers, lawes, and all things besides, that doe give any impediment unto their devices and complots.

I 3   Har-

Harding, Dorman, Stapleton, Sanders, Allen, Gregorie Martin, and divers other fugitives and Traytors, to make a more easie way, for the bringing in againe of poperie: have taken the like course in her highnesse time: meaning principally, by such vile slanders, to withdraw her Highnesse subjects, from their dutifull approbation of the present estate and reformation of Religion.

Goodman, Whittingham, Gilby, the author of the booke of obedience, with the rest of the *Geneva* complices in Queene *Maries* daies, practised the very same policie: when (as you have heard) according to the *Allobrogicall* resolution, they urged all states by degrees, rather to take armes, and to reforme Religion themselves by force, then to suffer such Idolatrie and superstition to remaine in the land.

But in these more politicall than Christian practices, as I said, that our English *disciplinarians* of these dayes, have far exceeded the *Scottish* Ministers: so may it be truely affirmed of them, that all the popish traitors, that hitherto have written, and all the said *Genevians* that then lived, so malitious and spitefull tauntes, for railing and bitter terms, for disdainfull and contemptuous speeches, did not come neere them.

Besides, it is especially to be observed, that in their own opinions, they have by these ungodly meanes so prevailed with the multitude, as that now they begin to vaunt and bragg of their good successe already therein attained. One of them sendeth us word from *Scotland*, that such as have withstood their pretended Church-government, *are made already in England to be despised and vile before all the people: that a poore simple Minister of theirs &c. heard with more reverence, and resorted unto with more dili-*

gent

gence, than one of ours; though he have the great bell rung, and men to helpe him up into the pulpit: that this was wrought by a contemptible, and very base and strange meanes, (meaning Martin and his sonnes libels, &c.) not once dreamed of by a thousand of Gods Saints: and that when their crosts, (meaning the Bishops) were set up, and they began to say all is ours, then their presumption was dashed, daunted, and taken downe.

They might as well have signified unto us, in what termes and reputation, her Majesty, her Parliaments, her Lords, her Judges, and her lawes, doe stand and hold with the people. In dealing as they have done, by their particular supplications and motions unto her Highnesse, and up to their Lords, their intents to that purpose, when the time shall serve (if in the meane while they be not prevented) are notably disclosed. For otherwise, it might have sufficed them, to have delivered their discontentments, in private manner, by writing, both to her Majesty, their Lords, and others in authority: thereby to have discharged their consciences without their publishing of them in Print to the world, except their purpose had likewise been, by that lewd meanes, to have brought them all into contempt, as well as the Bishops. What private man, if his friend should write a letter unto him, and lay open in the same, (either truly or falsly) many great crimes to his charge: and afterward should by Printing or any other waies publish it: could otherwise account of his dealing therein, but that he meant to make him thereby odious to the world, or at the least to be of no great account, or estimation.

Queene *Marie* was of nature and disposition, very mild and pitifull; and yet, because she suffered such cruelty and superstition to be practised and maintained in her days, you
have

have heard by the confistorian propositions (before mentioned) what was resolved by *Goodman, Whittingham, Gilby*, and the rest of the *Genevians* against her, concerning her deposition, &c. Which is a matter that would be well considered of, and in time provided for accordingly: considering that these our home-bred Sicophants, men of the *Geneva* mould, as proud and presumptuous as any that ever lived, do charge the present State, under her Majesty, (as before it is noted) with such great impiety, corruption, idolatry, superstition, and barbarous persecution: Which may touch her highnesse, as neerely (by their doctrine) for maintaining the present state, as Queene *Mary* was, for defending of Poperie.

Well, the conclusion of this Book is this, viz. that seeing our *English consistorians* do labour more vehemently, or at the least as eagerly, *per fas & nefas*, by slander, reproch, and malicious practices, to discredit all those, that withstand them, in their desires, for the *Geneva*-like discipline: as any other *Scottish* Ministers, Papists, or old *Genevians*, have laboured to discredit those, that maintained all kinde of Popery, Idolatry, and superstition, it is to be feared, least they proceed in the *Geneva* resolution, as their fellowes (whom they do imitate in Scotland, or rather whom they do excell) have done before them,

The end of the second Booke.

The third Book of Disciplinary Grounds and Practises.

Chap. I.

The practises of certaine English Reformers for Discipline, from the yeare, 1560. untill the yeare, 1572.

AS in *Scotland*, when they could not obtaine their desires, for the full establishing of their booke of Discipline, by lawfull authority; they procured such private subscription thereunto, as they were able, and so fell themselves to the practise of it (as ath beene said in the sixt chapter of the first Booke: even) have our men in *England*, of the same consort and fa‑ ion, proceeded in effect, upon the like occasion, for their w platforme: but yet in a different manner.

For the first ten or eleven years of her Majesties raigne, rough the peevish frowardnes, the outcries and excla‑ ations of those that came home from *Geneva*, against the rments prescribed to Ministers, and other such like mat‑ rs: no man (of any experience) is ignorant, what great ntention and strife was raysed: insomuch as their secta‑ s divided themselves from their ordinary congregati‑

K ons,

42 English Scottizing for Disciplinne by Practise. The 3 Book:

ons, and meeting together in private houses, in woods, and fields, had and kept there, their disorderly and unlawfull conventicles.

These kinds of assemblies (notwithstanding the inconvenience and absurdries of them in a Church reformed,) *M. Cartwright* (within a while after) tooke uppon him (in sort) to defend, saying: *that the name of conventicles, was too light and contemptuous for them.*

T.C. &c.
p. Pag. 5

About the twelfth yeare of her highnesse said government, these male contents growing weary of the foresaid dissentions, and being of restles dispositions, began to stir up new quarrels, concerning the *Geneva* Discipline: being the matter indeed which they still aymed at, in all their former proceedings. Hereupon, (the 14. of her Majesty) two *admonitions* were framed, and exhibited to the high Court of Parliament. The first contained their pretended griefes, with a declaration (forsooth) of the onely way to reforme them. vz. By admitting of that plat-forme; which was there described.

This admonition, finding small entertainement, (the authors or chiefe preferrers thereof being imprisoned) out commeth the second *admonition*, towardes the end of the same Parliament: with great lightning and thunder, as though heaven and earth should have met together; because of the little regard which was had before, to the former *admonition*. In this second *admonition*, the first is wholly justified: the Parliament (as it hath beene shewed) is mightily challenged: great words are vsed, and in plaine tearmes, it is there affirmed. That if they of that assembly would not then followe the advise of the first *admonition*, they would surely themselves be their owne carvers. *The Church* (say they) *may and must keepe God his orders: and surely this is only God his order,* (vz. the said platforme) *and ought*

Admoni-
con pag
&c.

to

The 3 *Book.* *English Scottizing for Discipline by Practise.* 43

to bee used in his Church, so that in conscience we are forced to speake for it, and to use it.

Whereupon, presently after the sayd Parliament, (vz. the twentieth of November, 1572.) there was a Presbytery erected at *Wandesworth in Surrey* (as it appeareth by a bill endorsed with *Master Fields* hand, thus: *the order of Wandesworth.*) In which order the Elders names, eleven of them, are set downe: the manner of their election is declared: the approuers of them, (one *Smith of Micham,* and *Crane of Roughamton*) are mentioned: their offices and certaine generall rules, (then given unto them to bee observed) were likewise agreed upon, and described.

Chap. II.
The secret meetings for Discipline, and the matters handled in them here in England from 1572 *till* 1583.

How they grew to bee so farre gone at *Wandesworth,* that I find not: they of *London,* at that time, were nothing so forward. And yet, as it appeareth by the lawfull deposition and oath of one, (then of that faction, but now a very honest man, a Batchellor of Divinitie, and an auncient Preacher) they had then their meetings of Ministers, tearmed brethren, in private houses in *London:* as namely of *Field, Wilcox, Standen, Iackson, Bonham, Seintloe, Crane,* and *Edmonds,* which meetings were called conferences, according to the plot in the first and second *admonitions* mentioned.

Tho Ed. both before the Commiss. and in the Star.Cham.

In these *London*-meetings, at the first, *little was debated, but against subscription, the attyre, and booke of common prayer. Marry after* (saith hee) *that Charke, Travers, Barber, Gardner,*

K 2 *Cheston,*

Cheston, and lastly Crooke and Egerton, joyned themselves into that brotherhood, then the handling of the Discipline began to be rife: then many motions were made, and conclusions were set downe. As for example.

That forasmuch, as divers bookes have beene written, and sundry petitions exhibited to her Majesty, the Parliament, their LL', and yet to little purpose: therefore every man should labour, by all the meanes he could, to bring into the Church, the said reformation themselves.

That the present government of the Church, by Arch-bishops & Bishops, was Antichristian: & that the only Discipline & governement of Christ, (as they termed it) viz. by Pastors, Doctors, Elders, and Deacons, should be established in place of the other.

That for the better bringing in of the said forme of Discipline, they should not onely, (aswell publikely as privately) teach it, but by little and little, as much as possibly they might, draw the same into practise, though they concealed the names, either of Presbytery, Elder, or Deacon, making little account of the name for the time, so that their offices might be secretly established.

There was an assembly of threescore Ministers, appointed out of Essex, Cambridge-shiere, and Norfolke, to meet the eighth of May, 1582. at Cockefield, (Master Knewstubs towne) there to conferre of the common booke, what might be tollerated, and what necessarily to be refused in every point of it: apparel, matter, forme, dayes, fastings, injunctions, &c.

Of this meeting it is thus reported. *Our meeting was appointed to be kept very secretly, and to be made knowne to none, &c.* That this assembly was also kept accordingly, it appeareth by these words. *Concerning the meeting, I hope all things were so proceeded in, as your selfe would like of: aswell for reverence to other brethren, as for other matters. I suppose before this time, some of the company, have told you by word: for that was permitted unto you.*

The 3 Book. *English Scottizing for Discipline by Practise.* 45

Another meeting was also appointed to be helde, that yeare, at the *Commencement* in *Cambridge*, as is plaine by these words. *Concerning the Commencement, I like well your motion: desiring it might so come to passe: and that it be procured, to be as generall as might be: which may easily be brought to passe, if you at London, shall so thinke well of it, and we here may understand your minde: we will (I trust) as we can, further it. M. Allen liketh well of the matter.*

Pig. to Field 1581

Chap. III.

A forme or booke of Discipline is drawne, and a resolution is agreed upon, how farre they might proceed from the practise of it, without breaking the peace of our Church.

Hilest the brethren in the Countrey, were comming thus fast on forward (as you have heard in the end of the former Chapter:) you must not thinke that the *Rabbies* in *London* were in the meane time idle. Hitherto it should seeme, that in all their former proceedings, they had relied chiefly, upon the first admonition and *Cartwrights* booke: as having had no particular and severall platforme, that was generally allowed of amongst them, for the Church of England. But now at the length (about the yeare, 1583.) the *forme of Discipline* (which is lately come to light) was compiled: and thereupon an assembly or Councell being helde (as I thinke at *London*, or at *Cambridge*) certaine decrees were made, concerning the establishing and the praise thereof. In which decrees, mention is made of a collection; concluded upon for the *Scottish* Ministers, fugitives here in *England*, 1583. (which sheweth the time when they were made) and order is likewise taken for the

K 3   putting

46 *English Scottizing for Discipline by Practise.* The 3 Book putting in use of the *Synodicall Discipline*; which also proveth the age of that booke.

The decrees themselves are extant to be seene, under Master *wights* hand; a man of that brotherhood. But it may not be omitted, that you must thinke; how the godly brethren in all these and such other their zealous courses, had never any meaning to disturbe the present state established. And thereupon (forsooth) in this conspiracy or councell mentioned, (like good and quiet spirited men) they had an especiall care, that the peace of the *Church* might not be broken, by any order or decree of theirs. So as then the question amongst them was, (seeing the Discipline must needs up) how farre they might proceed in the establishing and practise of it, keeping notwithstanding the peace of the *Church*, established already by her Majesty. And it was overruled accordingly, as it followeth in the decrees themselves, faithfully translated, word for word, out of their owne Latin coppy.

The title thereof, iz.

These be the things, that (doe seeme) may well stand with the peace of the Church.

The Decrees.

Let no man (though he be an University man) offer himselfe to the Ministery, nor let any man take upon him an uncertaine and vague Ministery, though it be offered unto him. But such as be called to the Ministery by some certaine Church, let them impart it unto that Classis *or* conference, *(whereof themselves are) or else unto some greater* Church assembly: *and if such shall be found fit by them, then let them be commended, by their letters unto the Bishop, that they may be ordained Ministers by him.*

These ceremonies in the Booke of common Prayer, *which being taken from* Popery, *are in controversie, doe seeme, that they ought*

ought to bee omitted and given over, if it may be done without danger, of being put from the Ministery. But if there be any imminent danger to be deprived, then this matter must be communicated with the Classis, in which that Church is: that by the judgement thereof, it may be determined, what ought to be done.

If subscription to the Articles of Religion, and to the book of common Prayer, shall be againe urged: it is thought, that the book of Articles, may be subscribed unto, according to the statute 13. Eliz. that is, unto such of them only, as containe the summe of Christian faith, and doctrine of the Sacraments. But for many weighty causes, neither the rest of the articles in that booke, nor the booke of common Prayer, may be allowed: no, though a man should be deprived of his Ministery for it.

It seemeth, that Church-wardens, and Collectors for the poore, might thus be turned into Elders and into Deacons.

When they are to be chosen, let the Church have warning fifteene dayes before, of the time of election, and of the ordinance of the Realme: but especially of Christs ordinance, touching appointing of watch-men and overseers in his Church: who are to foresee, that none offence or scandall doe arise in the Church: and if any shall happen, that by them it may be duly abolished.

And touching Deacons of both sorts (vz. men and women) the Church shall be monished, what is required by the Apostle: and that they are not to choose men, of custome and of course, or for their riches, but for their faith, zeale, and integrity: and that the Church is to pray, (in the meane time) to be so directed, that they make choice of men that be meet.

Let the names of such as are so chosen, be published, the next Lords day: and after that, their duties to the Church, and the Churches towards them, shall be declared: then let them be received unto the Ministery, to which they are chosen, with the generall prayers of the whole Church.

The Brethren are to be requested, to ordaine a distribution of

48 *English Scottizing for Discipline by Practise.* The 3 Book
all Churches, according to these rules (in that behalfe) that are set downe in the Synodicall Discipline, *touching* Classicall, Provinciall, Comitiall *or of* Commencements, *and* assemblies for the whole Kingdome.

The Classes *are to be required, to keep acts of memorable matters: which they shall see delivered to the* Comitiall *assembly, that frō thence they may be brought by the* provincial assembly.

Also, they are to deale earnestly with patrones, to present fit men: whensoever any Church is fallen void in that Classis.

The Comitiall *assemblies are to be monished, to make collections for reliefe of the poore and of Schollers: but especially for reliefe of such Ministers here, as are put out, for not subscribing to the Articles, tendred by the Bishops: also for reliefe of* Scottish *Ministers and others, and for other profitable and necessary uses.*

All the provinciall Synodes, *must continually, aforehand, foresee in due time: to appoint the keeping of their next* provinciall Synodes: *and for the sending of chosen persons, with certaine instructions, unto the* Nationall Synode *to be holden: whensoever the Parliament for the Kingdome shall be called, and at some certaine set time every yeare.*

Hitherto the *Decrees* of this grave *Councell*, whereby it seemeth to me, that when they resolved, they might proceede thus farre, and keepe (notwithstanding) the peace of the Church of *England* established: they opposed (in that resolution) the word *peace*, to *warre*: as though they should have agreed, how far they might runne on in this race, without urging of their followers, to force & armes. For otherwise, how could any sober men, so much as once have imagined, that they might, in this sort, overthrow (in effect) the present governement, and establish their own devises, and yet never breake the peace of the Church? But I will not presse this point. It is more agreeable to my purpose to pursue the chase.

Chap.

Chap. IV.

About the yeare 1581. they fell againe to the practice of their Discipline, and of a Consistorian question.

TO make good lawes, and not see them executed, is but labour lost. And therefore it should seeme, that these wise *Law-makers*, were presently after, as carefull to put the said orders in practice, as they were before to resolve upon them: as it may appeare by a letter, written to Master *Field* from *Antwerpe*, the 25. of *Iune*, 1583. by one *Cholmeley*, in answer of a former Letter, sent unto him from the said *Field*. For thus *Cholmeley* writeth: *Lator in tus & in corde, de meliori successu rerum vestrarum, quòd cum de conventibus vestris audiam, tum de Disciplinæ Ecclesiasticæ formali ordine multò libentißimè. Dicam quòd verum est, sero nimis incepistis: quisquis jam tandem vel incipere recusaveris, vel a tam præclaro incepto desistat, peccatum suum feret: pœnitendum est de priori lenitudine.* I am glad with all my heart, for the better successe of your affaires, not only in that I heare of your assemblies, but most willingly of all, in respect of your effectuall practising of the Ecclesiasticall Discipline. I will tell you that which is true, you have begun this course too too late. Whosoever shall now, either refuse to begin, or shall desist from so notable an enterprise, he shall beare his owne sin. You ought to repent you for your former slownes. And afterward, thus out of the same Letter, to incourage Master *Field* and the brethren. *In nulla re terreamini ab iis qui se opponunt, quod illis quidem est exitii indicium, vobis autem salutis, idque a Deo.* In nothing feare your adversaries, which is to them a token of perdition, but to you of salvation, and that from God.

In *July* the next year, vz. 1584. some of the *Scottish* ministers

Philip. 2:

Gelibrand to Field.

nisters afore spoken of, went to the *Act in Oxford:* where Master *Gelibrand* with his brethren, gave them great entertainment. At that time, there was a notable question propounded amongst their favourers there, by the said Ministers, as is manifest by these words. *Here have beene a good company of godly brethren this Act.* Master *Fen, Wilcox, Axton: the Scottish ministers, and we have had some meeting and conference to our great comfort that are here. One point (which then was moved) I would wish to be throughly debated among you and them, concerning the prooceeding of the Minister in his dutie, without the assistance or tarrying for the Magistrate, &c.*

What was resolved amongst the brethren of *London*, about this matter at that time, I know not. Marry this I finde, that presently thereupon, they grew more violent, and prepared themselves to proceede more resolutely, in the challenging of their Discipline, as it is plaine by the dealing both of them, and of their favourers, that yeare in *November* and *December* after, at the *Parliament*, 27. of her Majestie.

And besides, let the said Master *Gelibrands* words, in a Letter to *Field*, dated the 12. of *Ianuary* after, vz. 1584. be considered. For (as it seemeth to me) they either tend to sedition, or to the admitting, in *Oxford*, of the foresaid *Decrees* or *Discipline*. Sure I am, that they can hardly (for ought I see) receive any good construction. Thus he writeth,

I have already entred into the matters, whereof you write, and dealt with three or foure severall Colleges, concerning those among whom they live. I finde, that men are very dangerous in this point, generally favouring reformation: but when it cometh to the particular point, some have not yet considered of these things, for which others in the Church are so much troubled: others

Book 3. *English Scottizing for Discipline by Practice.*

thers are afraid to testifie any thing with their hands, lest it breed danger before the time. And after: *many favour the cause of reformation, but they are not Ministers, but young students, of whom there is good hope, if it be not cut off by violent dealing before the time. As I heare by you, so I meane to go forward, where there is any hope, and to learne the number, and to certifie you thereof.*

Furthermore, at the time of the *Parliament* last mentioned, I finde, that there was a *nationall Synod* held likewise in *London* by these brethren: according to their former decisions and *Synodicall* Discipline. This appeareth by three letters. The first was, from *eleven Ministers of Essex*, to *Field*: wherin they desire to *be certified, whether the brethren meant to be exercised in prayer and fasting, and upon what day.* 26. Ian. 1584.
The second was, from *nine of the said* Ministers, to *Field* and *Clark*: wherin they writ thus: *We have elected two godly and faithfull brethren, M. Wright, and M. Gifford, to joyne with you in that businesse.* 2. Febr. 1584.
The third was, from *Gelibrand*, to *Field*: Wherein he excuseth himselfe of a great oversight, in these words. *Touching my departure from that holy assembly without leave, &c. I crave pardon, both of you and them, &c.* And thus (saith he) *commending this holy cause to the Lord himselfe, and your godly counsaile to the President thereof, I take my leave.* 29. Novemb. 1584.

CHAP. V.

Their Book of Discipline is reviewed: it was after sent abroad about 1587. it was put in practice, in Northamptonshire, and many other places.

Notwithstanding that the Booke of Discipline was abroad, as it hath beene noted, (in the third Chapter,) and that the brethren had framed themselves (as they might) unto the rules thereof: yet

there

76 *English Scottizing for Discipline by Practice.* Book 3.

there were found some imperfections in it: which in the *Synod*, mentioned in the former chapter, (as I take it) were referred to Maister *Travers*, to be corrected and ordered by him, as his leisure will permit. Which appeareth by a letter of Maister *Fields* to Maister *Travers*, in these words.

Field to Travers, 3. Iuly. 1585.
Concerning our other businesse: I would wish, that the Discipline were read over with as much speed as could be, and that some good directions were given, for the brethren abroad, who are earnest to enter some good course for the furtherance of the Lords cause. And after in the same place: *I find many abroad, very willing to joyne with the best, to put in practice that which shall be agreed upon by the brethren. If it might please the brethren therefore, that those or the like instructions (which we had) with a perfect copie of the Discipline, might be sent, I would wholly imploy my selfe in that service.* Another also upon the longer stay thereof. *I pray you hasten the forme of Discipline and send it.*

Gelibrand to Field, 9. of Novem. 1585.
And the same man againe: *I pray you remember the forme of Discipline, which* M. Travers *promised to make*

Gelibrand to Field, 30. Ianuary.
perfect, and send it me when it is finished. We will put it in practice, and trie mens minds therein, as we may.

According to these requests, the draught of Discipline was at the last finished, and then sent abroad, to be approved generally by all the brotherhood, as may thus appeare.

Gelibrand to Field.
The discipline we have received, and we give you and the brethren hearty thanks for it. As yet we are not resolved in all points of it, having had but small time to peruse it, nor the commodity of often meeting about it. But we have taken order for our monethly assembly, and after our owne consents yeelded unto it, for associating other into our company, whom we shall thinke approved. And another. *We heartily give God thanks*

Sander to Field, 20. Iune, 1587.
(saith one) *for the godly and most Christian paines of the brethren, in the travaile of the Discipline: which is come to our hand*

Book 3. *English Scottizing for Discipline by Practice.*

hands to be considered of *Gelibrands* letter of his receit of the book of Discipline, was written in the name of the brethren in *Oxford*. At which time there was another Synod held in *London: Whither* (saith the letter) *Maister* West *and Maister* Browne *were sent from* Oxford: *to whom they referred the estate of their Church, to be related: and by whom they desired to understand directions from the Synod, how they might deale afterwards in those matters.*

Within a while after, viz. 1587. (as I suppose) there was in like sort an *assembly or Synod held of the* Cambridgeshire *brotherhood:* accompanied peradventure with some of other shires. About which time also, upon the new edition of the foresaid book, the further practice of the *Discipline* mentioned by *Cholmeley,* 1583. (as is before shewed) began to spread it selfe more freely, into the most parts of the *Realme:* but especially (for ought I do yet understand) it was most friendly entertained amongst the Ministers of *Northamptonshire*, as it appeareth in record by some of their owne depositions, 16. of May, 1590. in these words following. *About two yeares and a halfe since the whole shire was divided into three Classes.* 1. *The Classis of* Northamptonshire, *consisting of these Ministers:* M. Snape, M. Penry, M. Sibthorpe, M. Edwards, M. Littleton, M. Bradshaw, M. Larke, M. Fleshware, M. Spicer, &c. 2. *The Classis of* Daventry *side, consisting of these:* M. Barebon, M. Rogers, M. King, M. Smart, M. Sharp, M. Prowdloe, M. Elliston, &c. 3. *The Classis of* Kettring *side: consisting of these:* M. Stone, M. Williamson, M. Fawsbrook, M. Patinson, M. Massey, &c.

This device (saith *Maister Iohnson*) *is commonly received in most* *parts of England,* (as I have heard in sundry of our meetings:) *but especially in* Warwickshire, Suffolke, Norfolke, Essex, &c.

This appeareth under M. Wights hand.

M. Iohnson. So in effect M. Littleton, M. Sharpe.

* M. Snape reported as much, as Edward Smith, Ri. Hawgar, and Ri. Holme have deposed.

L 3 The

The manner of every particular Classis is this. At * their meeting (which is alwaies in some private house, but yet in their Mother Cities) first a moderator is chosen, in this sort: One of them conceiveth a prayer, for Gods direction in that choice.

*M. Sharpe and M. Littleton do likewise herein agree with M. Iohnson.

Then he, that conceived the prayer, sitteth alone in scrutinie: and every one giveth his voice secretly unto him. He that hath most voices is chosen.

The moderator, thus chosen, conceiveth another prayer: that God would blesse him in the course of his office. Then being set at the tables end, with his brethren by him, the names of all the brethren are called. If any were absent at their first sitting down, he sitteth after in order, as he commeth, for avoiding of superiority.

The authority of the moderator endureth untill the next meeting of that Classis. At the breaking up of every Classis, there is ever some certaine time appointed, when they shall meet againe: which is somtime within a fortnight, but commonly three weeks at the farthest: If any thing do fall out in the meane time, fit to be consulted upon: the moderator may call the Classis together sooner, according to an order made amongst themselves.

*M. Littleton deposeth as much.

It is * a generall order, that when any is admitted into a Classis, he doth promise under his hand, that he will submit himselfe, and be obedient to all such orders and decrees, as shall be set down by the same Classis to be observed.

As for example: these were part of the particular articles, whereunto every one of Northampton Classis did subscribe, at his entring or admittance into it: we do promise to submit our selves unto such orders and decrees, as shall be set downe by our Classis: We do promise to submit our selves, to be censured by our brethren of this Classis, in all matters concerning doctrine and Discipline, &c.

In this Classis it was furthermore concluded and agreed upon, that when any controversie did arise, touching any matters of doctrine, or about the interpretation of any place of Scriptures, every

Book 3. *English Scottizing for Discipline by Practice.* 79

every one of that Claſſis, ſhould alwayes yeeld therein, unto that interpretation and reſolution, which the brethren of that Claſſis ſhould determine of. And ſo alſo when any queſtions did riſe amongſt them of greater difficultie. As for Example, Maſter Stone mooved this queſtion to the Northampton Claſſis in the behalfe of one: vz. two are contracted, one of them marrieth with a third, he or ſhe ſo married are free againe. The queſtion is, whether the former contract, doe now againe binde. And the reſolution was, it did not: which was a falſe reſolution.

The determinations and acts concluded upon in this Claſſis, were regiſtred in a booke by Snape: choſen Regiſter by the companie, and who alwaies kept the ſame. *M. Sharpe to the ſame purpoſe of Daventry Claſſis.*

Beſides thoſe particular Claſſes, there is another kind of meeting, which is termed the Aſſembly. And it conſiſteth (for example) in Northamptonſhire, of the number of ſix, that is two of every Claſſis, which are ſent thither by election. The ordinary place of this aſſembly in Northamptonſhire, was at Northampton, where Snape commonly was one, and a chiefman, Barbon and King, were the men that came uſually from Daventry ſide: and Stone and Williamſon from Kettring ſide.

At the meeting of the ſix, there is alwayes a moderator firſt choſen, in manner and forme, as in the Claſſis: and ſo likewiſe for their further order of proceeding. The moderator continueth his authority, over all the three Claſſes, untill the like meeting happen againe: which is never certain. But yet comonly within ſix or eight weeks, upon occaſion ſignified from the Claſſes unto this moderator. For unto him belongeth the calling of this aſſembly.

The matters, which here are handled, are thoſe of great moment; ſuch as concerne the ſtate of the Church generally. As for example: the writing of letters to the brethren at Oxford, Cambridge, and London, to certifie them of their proceedings, and to know what courſe is held amongſt them, in thoſe places, for the *The like M. Sharpe of Daventry Claſſis.*

the *Discipline* and *government*, which they terme Reformation:) to the intent, that the particular Classes, upon their advertisements, may direct themselves, and their Churches accordingly.

It is likewise alwaies concluded, at such times, which of the six assembled shall pen the letters. And in this choice, Snape was commonly the man.

The men to whom they usually did write: were one in Cambridge; Travers in London, and Gelibrand in Oxford. When any answers were returned from those places: they were commonly directed to Snape, or to him that had written to them in the name of the brethren.

Two especiall points (I remember) were concluded in this assembly: the one was, for a survey of all the Churches in Northamptonshire: th'other, for an order to be observed at the last Parliament, which then drew neere.

M. Snape to the same purpose of Diventrie Classis.

The survey was, to know what every benefice in the shire was worth, how many soules by a generall conjecture, were in every parish: who were the incumbents, and of what life, paines and qualities they were. To this purpose, the fittest men, and such as were best acquainted in the shire were nominated: as Litleton for Haddon Deanerie, &c. Which dutie he performed for his part to the uttermost: and brought a most railing discourse, against every Minister, which was not of our companie.

The end propounded of this survey, was vz. that if upon signification to the brethren abroad, what was done there: they would likewise make the like survey in other countries: the Parliament (if need required) and to the better furthering of their purposes, might have a generall view, of all the Ministers in England that impugned their desires.

The second point before mentioned was this: vz. a conclusion to send up to London, one or two of every Classis in Northhamptonshire, with letters of credit, to attend at the Parliamen

Book 3. *English Scottizing for Discipline by Practice.* 81

ment: to joyne themselves with the brethren of other countries: and to offer disputation, (if it should be so thought meet) and to undertake any other such matter, as should then and there be determined of amongst them: and that there should be letters written of this resolution, to know how the brethren abroad liked it: or what other course they would hold at that time, for the bringing in of Discipline and Church government.

These two points, were penned by Snape: and sent to the brethren abroad, as it was ordered.

What answer was returned to Snape, from the brethren in Oxford and Cambridge, I know not: but well I remember, that Travers did write to Snape, a very cunning Letter: wherein he shewed himself not to mislike the foresaid survey to be generally made, but signified, that the Parliament drawing on so fast, it could not be done so soone. But for the second point: that (he writ) was liked, and meet to be followed.

Whereupon the Classes of Northamptonshire, did send up some three or foure, as Settle for Northampton, Rogers for Daventry, &c. with a further conclusion, that if any of them (upon occasion) should be committed, others should be sent up in their places.

Although the time was short, for the generall accomplishing of those forenamed points: yet this examinate thinketh, something was done in the first: viz. as he hath heard, a survey was made to the purpose before touched, of the Ministers in Northfolke, Suffolke and Essex. And for the second, true it was, that many were sent to attend at the Parliament, from the most parts of England. And one resolution was, that some twenty or thirty of them, should have come in their gownes, with all gravitie, to the Parliament-house-doore; and there have desired by petition a disputation.

This survey hath beene made in the most shires of England: as by the survey themselves to be shewed it appeareth. They are in manner of Lea-chemish libels.

Furthermore, concerning some censures used, there was a generall consent and purpose, amongst the brethren, touching a secret

M

M　　cret

ret kinde of excommunication: for examples sake. A lay man committeth some sinne. One of the Elders was to admonish him. The partie is obstinate. The Elder must take two or three with him the second time. And if this serve not, then he is to be debarred from the communion. In this case, if the said partie should (notwithstanding) intrude himselfe to communicate, then it was agreed to repell him upon pretence of certaine words in the communion booke. So as thereby, they might keep their own course, for their Discipline, and yet have a cloak to cover them withall, out of the book.

Againe, another thing is notable to this effect. About a yeare and a halfe agoe, John Nelson of Northampton, an Elder or a Deacon of Saint Peters, (as I think) having either his daughter or his sister gotten with childe, in his house, by one of his servants, Master Snape dealt with the said servant, to urge him to publike repentance: and at the last, so farre prevailed with him (as it was thought,) that he promised the next Sunday so to doe: but came not. Whereupon Snape made a very bitter Sermon against him. The next Sunday he came indeed. And then Snape made a long prayer, that God would give him grace, to make a faithfull acknowledgement of his sinne &c. That done the penitentiary made publike confession &c. Which being performed, Snape absolved him; and then entred into a great discourse how cleare the partie was, and free from that sinne committed, even as though he had been newly born: charging the congregation that no man should presume, at any time after, to object the same unto him. But that, which was most wondred at: whereas this poore man was thus dealt withall, Snape caused lame Prettie, a Souldier of Barwicke (who without any calling in the Church at all, saving that he had a toleration to read, did such service in that place, as was appointed by Snape to be read, till he came to Church) the next morning to marrie the said penitentiary to the woman with childe before named, without any

bring

Book 3. *English Scottizing for Discipline by Practice.* 83

bringing of her, unto any such publike repentance. Hereof grew amongst the people great speech, that the poore man was so used, and the richer mans sister or daughter was so freed. The said lame Souldier, hath married many in that place, upon Snapes commandement: for that Snape holdeth, that duty to appertaine no more to the Ministers office, than to any other man.

And as touching that point mentioned, of the brethrens submitting of themselves, by subscription, to be censured in their *Classis*: it was thus used in the *Northampton Classis*. The brethren being together in a chamber, the party to be first censured, (as they were all to be in course) goeth forth out of the chamber. Then the moderator asketh every mans opinion of him: how he behaveth himselfe aswell in his life, as in his *Ministery*: and every man, having spoken his opinion, the party is called in: and then, if he were not any way touched, he is greatly commended: if otherwise, then reproved, as the causes require. For example, Edwards of Cortnall comming under this censure, was blamed for using the Crosse in Baptisme: and at his comming-in againe, was wonderfull sharpely dealt withall for the same.

Thus farre *Maister Iohnson* of the *Northampton Classis*. With whom do also agree in the principall points: *Maister Littleton*, as touching the same *Classis*, *Maister Sharp*, and *Maister Walker*, Preachers and persons deposed, concerning the *Classis* of *Daventry* side: and *Maister Stone* (a Preacher likewise) upon his oath, for that of *Kettring* side. One or two points I may not omit, which *Maister Stone* hath delivered. He confesseth *that at diverse times,* *Maister* Snape, *Maister* Barbon, *Maister* Sharpe, *Maister* Prowdloe, *Maister* King, *Maister* Johnson, *Maister* Sibthorp, *Maister* Spicer, *Maister* Baxter, *Maister* Littleton, *Maister* Williamson, *Maister* Bradshaw, *Maister* Fleshware, *Maister* Harrison, *and hee, have met in* Northampton: *And likewise at*

Stone in the Starchamber

M 2 Kettring

Kettring: *and at his house, the most of them, with some others, as* Maister *Rishbrooke*, Maister Atkinson, Maister Davyes, Maister Massye, Maister Okes *&c. about matters of discipline.* And he saith farther, *that in an assembly had, either at his house or at* Kettring, *it was propounded, treated, and concluded, that the Apocrypha writings were not to be read in the Church.* And in another assembly, which of them he doth not remember, he affirmeth likewise, *That it was debated and concluded upon, that the superiority of the Bishops of this land, over the rest of the Ministers, is not warranted by the Word of God.*

To these depositions, concerning the *Northamptonshire Classes*, I might add the depositions of one maister *Parker*, Vicar of *Dedham* in *Essex*, for the proofe of the *Classes* in that shire: as of one about *Brayntree side*, consisting of these Ministers, Maister *Calverwell*, Maister *Rogers*, Maister *Gifford*, *&c*. another about *Colchester*, consisting of these Ministers, Doctor *Chapman*, Doctor *Chricke*, Maister *Dowe*, Maister *Farrar*, Maister *Newman*, Maister *Tey*, &c. and so likewise the depositions of others.

Hen. Asker to Field. Apr. 14. 1583.

Ego singulis sabbatis, si non alius adveniens locum suppleat, cum præscripta leiturgias formula nihil habens commertii, in cœtu concionem habeo: idque reverendorum fratrum consilio, qui suos habent singulis ferè hebdomadis conventus, qui etiam me in eorum numerum, (sic est mihi propitius Deus) benignè ascripserunt. I preach every Sabbath day, (if no other that commeth by chance, doth supply the place) having nothing to doe at all with the forme or booke of Common Prayer: and that by the counsell of the reverend brethren, who have their meetings almost every week, who have also (God being so mercifull unto me) admitted me very kindly into their number.

But in following of that course, I should be too tedious. I will only set down one mans witnesse more, agreeing

ing with Master *Iohnson*, for the proof, that the like *Classes* are or have been held in most Shires in England: and so referring you to judge of them all, by that of *Northampton*, I will go forward.

About two yeares since, Maister *Snape* did say and affirme, in the presence of *Edward Smith, Robert Vicars, Edward Bird, Richard Holmes,* and himselfe, *that there were three or foure small* Classes *of Ministers in every shire, where there were any learned Preachers, who did use (in their meetings) to debate of the Discipline, by Pastors, Doctors, Elders, and Deacons, and that the said severall small* Classes, *did send their resolutions and opinions, to the greater assemblies at* Cambridge *at* Sturbridge *Fayre time, and at* London *at* Bartholomew *Fayre time, which did meet together also for the same purpose: & that if the said great* assembly *did like of that, which was done by the smaller* Classes, *then was the same (so liked of) generally concluded, to be that, which ought to be, or stand, in the Church.* (As for example.) *That it was concluded and agreed upon, both in the said* Classicall *and* generall assemblies, *that the dumb ministery was no ministery, or els no lawfull ministery: and that the Ministers in their severall charges, should all teach one kind of doctrine, tending to the erecting of the aforesaid government by* Pastors, Doctors, Elders *and* Deacons: *which points* (saith *Holmes* of himselfe in another examination) *were concluded in the Synod at* Sturbridge *Fayre last. viz.* 1588.

Chap. VI.

A Synod is held at Coventry, 1588. *many questions are resolved, the book of Discipline is subscribed unto.*

THere is mention made, in the last chapter, of a Synod or meeting, 1587. of the *Cambridgeshire Classicall* Ministers, and peradventure of some others also with them. In which meeting there were certaine questions

stions propounded and dealt in: the which questions were afterwards sent by their direction, to the *Warwickshire Classes*, or brethren assembled in those parts, to be farther intreated of and resolved.

The next yeare after, viz. 1588. the said *Warwickshire Classes, &c.* assembling themselves together, in councell, (as it seemeth at *Coventry*,) the questions mentioned, were determined upon: and besides, other matters were also concluded, as by the acts themselves following (to be shewed under *Maister Wights* hand, and are acknowledged in effect upon two mens oathes in the *Starre-Chamber*) may sufficiently appeare. Thus the proceedings of that meeting are intituled. *Acta conventus Classium Warwic, die decimo quarto 1588. The Acts of the assembly of the Warwickshire Classes the tenth day of the fourth moneth. And touching the question specified. Quæstiones à fratribus ex Synodo Cantabrigiensi, anno superiore delatæ, eâ quæ sequitur formula sunt explicatæ.* The questions brought the other yeare from the brethren of the Cambridge Synod, are resolved in manner as followeth. I will not trouble my paper with the forme which they used, but these were some of their resolutions: viz.

That private Baptisme is unlawfull.

That it is not lawfull to read Homilies in the Church.

That the signe of the Crosse is not to be used in Baptisme.

That the faithfull ought not to communicate with unlearned ministers, although they may be present at their service, if they come of purpose to heare a Sermon. The reason is, because lay men, aswell as Ministers, may read publike Service.

That the calling of Bishops &c. is unlawfull.

That as they deale in causes Ecclesiasticall, there is no duty belonging unto them, nor any, publikely to be given them.

That it is not lawfull, to be ordained by them into the ministery; or to denounce either suspensions or excommunications sent from them.   That

Book 3.   *English Scottizing for Discipline by Practice.*   87

That it is not lawfull, to rest in the Bishops deprivation of any from the ministerie, except (upon consultation with the neighbour-ministers adjoyning, and his flocke) it seeme so good unto them: but that he continue in the same, untill he be compelled to the contrary by civill force.

That it is not lawfull, to appeare in a Bishops Court: but with protestation of their unlawfulnesse.

That Bishops are not to be acknowledged, either for Doctors, Elders, *or* Deacons, *as having no ordinary calling.*

That touching the restauration of their Ecclesiasticall discipline, it ought to be taught to the people, data occasione, *as occasion should serve.*

That nondum (*as yet*) *the people are not to be solicited,* publicè (*publikly*) *to the practice of the discipline:* donec, (*till*) *they be better instructed in the knowledge of it.*

That men of better understanding, are to be allured privatly, to the present imbracing of the Discipline and practice of it, as far as they shall be well able, with the peace of the Church. And thus far the *provinciall Synode* of the *Warwickeshire Classis.*

Likewise at that time, there was in the same assembly, a great approbation obtained of the foresaid booke of *Discipline,* as to be a *draught of Discipline, essential and necessary for all times:* and certaine articles (being devised in approbation, and for the manner of the use of that book,) were then brought forth, treated of, and subscribed unto,) as Master *Nutter* and Master *Clevely,* two that were then present, have deposed,) by Master *Cartwright,* Master *Fenne,* Master *Wight, &c.* who promised to guid themselves by the said discipline, and according to it, as it is set downe in the said articles, which hereafter shall be likewise declared. It apeareth also by the said parties depositions, that divers others did subscribe at the same time, (or at the least within a short time after,) but they might not (forsooth) by reason of their

Nutter and Cleveley in the Star-chamber.

owne

owne consciences, name them. Howbeit the matter is otherwise plaine enough, who they were: by a note taken with *Master Littelton: vz. Iohn Oxenbridge, Edward Gillibrand, Hercules Clevely, Anthony Nutter, Leonard Fetherstone, Mathew Hulme, Edward Lord, &c.*

This booke, having thus at the last received this great allowance, more authentically: was carried far and nere, for a generall ratification of all the brethren. It was offered to the *Daventry side* Classis, as *Master Sharp and Master Walker* have deposed; and likewise at *Northampton by Penry*, as *Master Littleton* affirmeth. But that which master *Iohnson* hath set downe is worthy the remembrance. The effect of it, is this: *That when the book of Discipline came to Northampton to be subscribed unto: there was a generall censuring used amongst the brethren there, as it were to sanctifie themselves partly by sustaining a kinde of penance, and reproof for their former conformity to the orders of the Church, established by her Majesty, and other matters of conversation: and partly to prepare their minds for the devout accepting of the foresaid booke.* In which course of censuring used at that time, there was such ripping up, one of anothers life, even from their youth, as that they came unto great bitternesse, with many *reviling termes* amongst themselves, one growing thereby odious to another, and some did *thereupon utterly forsake those kinde of assemblies.*

Sharpe and Walker before the Commissioners.

Iohnson before the Commissioners.

Chap. VII.

The book of the pretended Discipline is made perfect at Cambridge: certaine Synods are kept: and of their estimation.

IT might have beene deemed, that after so many viewes, *Synods*, and subscriptions, this worthy draught of discipline, would have growne to great

Booke. 3. *English Scottizing, for Discipline by Practise.* 89

great perfection: but it falleth out otherwise. For (as it is confessed upon oath) at *Sturbridge fayre*-time, the next yeare (after the said *Classicall* councell of the *Warwickshire* brethren) vz. in the yeare, 1589. there was another Synode or generall meeting, held *in Saint Iohns Colledge in Cambridge.* Where (saith M. Barber) *they did correct, alter, and amend divers imperfections contained in the booke, called* Disciplina ecclesiæ sacra, verbo Dei descripta: *and* (as master *Stone* affirmeth) *did not onely perfect the said forme of Discipline, but also did then and there,* (as he remembreth,) *voluntarily agree amongst themselves, that so many as would should subscribe to the said booke of Discipline after that time.* The persons, that met in this assembly, were (as these two last deponents affirme.) *master Cartwright, master Snape, master Alkon, master Gifford, master Perkins, master Stone, master Barber, master Harrison, with others, &c.*

I find mention also of another Synode, 1589. held (as I take it) at *Ipswich.* Thus one *Iohn Warde* did write, that yeare, to certaine at *Ipswich: I thinke not to come over, till the Synode, which is* (as I take it) *a moneth after Michaelmas.*

It hath beene observed before, out of master *Edmonds* deposition: cap. 2. who were the *Classicall* brethren of *London.* It is also fit to be understood, who they are, that most commonly met there also, at their more *generall, provinciall* or *nationall* assemblies or Synodes. And this both *master Barber,* and *master Stone,* doe sufficiently declare. *For the space of about foure yeares last past,* (saith master Barber,) *and since the last Parliament* (saith master Stone,) *there have bin severall meetings in* London *at the houses of master Gardiner, master Egerton, master Travers, and master Barber. The persons, that usually mett in these assemblies,* (saith master Barber,) *were master Cartwright, master Charke, master Travers, master Egerton, master Gardiner, master Oxenbridge,*

N

master Gelibrand, master Culverwell, master Browne of Oxford, master Allen, master Gifford, master Sommerscales, and himselfe.

Master Cartwright, master Travers, and master Egerton, were at sundry times chosen Moderators or Presidents *in the said assemblies*. And afterwards generally of the office of the Moderators. *The resolutions, conclusions, and determinations of such matters, as were disputed of, and agreed upon, by the more number of them, that so disputed in the said assemblies: were by the said* Moderators or Presidents, *before named, at the times and places of the said severall assemblies, summarily and briefly, either written in a booke, or otherwise set downe in loose papers, as to the said* Moderators, or Presidents *should bee thought meet or convenient.*

As the *Classicall* assemblies of *London* were of greater estimation, then those in the Countrey: so these more generall meetings or Synods last mentioned, were of highest authority: and indeed the *grandest* of all the rest. It may be said truely of them both, that they have been the kindling sparkes of all those flames, which are in the Church. What was there ordered, went, as perfectly currant. From thence, the brethren, of other places, did fetch their light. As doubts did arise, thither they were sent to be resolved. The *Classicall* and *Synodicall decrees* in other places, were never authenticall indeed, (as it seemeth,) till there they were ratified. The chiefest directions, for all the brethren elsewhere, were sent from thence. It is wonderfull to consider, how men so obstinate and wilfull in their owne wayes against the Church of *England*, established by her Maiestie; should be brought to submit themselves in such sort, as they did, to be led by these assemblies, as elswhere it doth appeare.

CHAP.

Chap. VIII.

Vpon some detecting of the premisses some were called into question: they refused to be examined: al they were charged, which is in effect confessed.

IN the yeare, 1590. upon the detecting (before some of her *Majesties Commissioners in causes Ecclesiasticall*) of the most of these things, whereof I have hitherto spoken: *Interrogatories* were drawen, containing in them the effect of all the premisses ; and divers such Ministers were sent for, as were sayd to have beene the cheife ringleaders in all those actions, Accordingly they appeared: but in the place when they should be examined, they refused to answere upon their oaths. Divers pretences therof were made, as one; that first they would see the *Interrogatories*, whereof they should be examined. The generall summe of them, was imparted unto them: as it was likewise told them, that they should bee charged to answere no further, then by the lawes of the Realme they were bound to doe. But all this would not serve. Whereupon the *Interrogatories* themselves were shewed unto some, as namely to *Master Snape*, who stood most at the first upon that point, and did pretend, that if first hee might see them, he would then answere unto them. But the issue was accordingly, as it was expected: For having perused them, he was further off, then he was before: and writt to his friends, what was the summe of them : to the intent they might *be forewarned*, and so (as he sayd) *become better armed.* Which course taken by him: was not without the great providence of God. For thereby their whole plot, and all in effect, that was laid to their charges, was discovered. His Letters were intercepted,

In the Preface

wherein

wherein he writeth after this sort.

Snape to N.N. 1590.

Reverend and beloved, this day Aprill the 7. I have been againe before the Commissioners: After much adoe, I obtained to see and peruse the Articles against me, (but briefly and in their presence onely,) they are many, (36. 37. besides those under mine owne hand,) and very large, some twelve, some twenty lines long, consisting of many branches. As far as I could (for the time) conceive and remember, they may be referred to these two heads: some concerning my selfe, together with others, and some touching my selfe alone. The former sort are touching Classes *and* Synodes: *wherein there are mentioned particular places: (London, Oxford, Cambridge:) times (* Act, Commencement, Sturbridge fayre, Tearme: *) persons, (* Cartwright, Perkins, Travers, Charke, Egerton, Barbon, Stone, Snape, Knewstub, Allen, Dike, *& divers others, &c.) and some things dealt in and agreed upon, &c.* By all which, besides many other things specified, it is most evident, that they have manifest and certaine knowledge, not onely of generals, but also of specials and particulars.

Snape to Barbon Aprill 11. 1590. and so also to Stone.

Beloved, I have twise appeared before the high Commissioners, the first time, the issue was prison: the second, close prison. This is my state now: the causes of both, and the proceedings in both, you shall receive of Master Knightlye, *the former more large in a Dialogue, the latter more briefly in a Letter: both imperfect, both imperused: read them, and returne them with what speed you may: for I have now no coppy of them: let them be wisely kept, lest they breed more anger. I have procured another coppy to be sent to Master* Stone, *that in both places you might be forewarned, & forearmed. Touching the conferences, those of our Countrey, are yet more particularly discovered: persons (besides those there named)* Kinge, *of* Coleworth: Prowdloe, *of* Weeden, *&c.* Spicer, *of* Cogenho: Edwardes, *of* Cortenhall, *&c. places:* Sharpes *house at* Fawsley: Snapes *chamber at* Northampton

ton, &c. *Si quis conjecturæ sit locus: I would judge* Iohn Iohnson *to have beene the man: because (to my remembrance) persons and things of his time being mentioned, hee onely is not named. Whosoever and howsoever, wee see the Lord calleth us to be more resolute. They will not, they cannot be any longer concealed: now whether it be better and more safe, that one man with the consent of the rest, should boldly, freely, and wisely, confesse, and lay open, &c. or that some weake (or wicked) man should without consent, and in evill sort acknowledge, &c. Iudge you: the thing they ayme at, is, A conventicle. It must come to tryall. In the cause of murther, &c. It is wont to be enquired, whether the party fled upon it: consider and apply to this matter, and the Lord give us wisdome in all things. It were good you sent to* T. C. *with speed.*

Chap. IX.

Cartwright is called for, by authority: a Synod is held in London, it is there resolved that he shall refuse to be examined upon his oath.

Afterward the same yeare before mentioned, 1590. (in *September*, as I take it) Master *Cartwright* upon occasion was sent for, by the said Commissioners. Now, *about a weeke or a fortnight before*, Cartwright *was committed,* (sayth Master *Stone*) *whereas, the question mentioned by* Snape *to* Barrow *& the brethren: (which, as it seemeth, troubled them all:) vz. whether it were not fit, that one man with the consent of the rest, should boldly, freely, and wisely, confesse and lay open &c. came to be disputed in London.* There was a Synode or meeting, held at Master *Gardiners*, by these brethren, Master Cartwright, Master Charke, Master Travers, Master Egerton, Master Gardiner, Master Barbon, Master Barber,

Depos. in the Star chamber.

master

master Oxenbridge, *master* Gelibrand, *master* Culverwel, *my selfe, and certaine other Ministers: and they did then and there debate and consider amongst themselves, whether it were fit or convenient, that the said master* Cartwright, *(after his commitment to prison) should discover or reveale, all or any the matters, which passed in conference and disputation, in any of their former assemblies, or not.* What the resolution hereof was, whether through the examiners oversight, or Master *Stones* perversnesse, (I know not) but it is not set downe. Howbeit the effects which followed, do make it manifest.

For master *Cartwright*, about the time before limited, being convented: and moved in the Consistory at *Paules*, by the *Bishop* of London, the then two *Lords cheife Iustices*, master Iustice *Gawdy*, master *Sergeant Puckering, now Lord Keeper of the great Seale of England*, master *Attorney Generall now Lord Cheife Iustice of England*: and divers others her Maiesties Commissioners then present to take his oath to answere to certaine *Interrogatories*: yet notwithstanding that the cheife points of them were then delivered in generall tearmes unto him, & that the said both honourable and grave persons, did (every man) severally assure him upon their credits, that by the lawes of the Realme he was bound to take his oath, & thereupon to answere, as he was required: he desired to be borne withall, and said that hee thought he was not bound by the lawes of God so to doe.

Chap. X.
Further proof for their practice of their Discipline: collected out of the rules of their subscribed booke.

IF hitherto, as yet the point (I have in hand) be not sufficiently prooved: vz. that our *English reformers* have attempted after the *Scottish* Ministers fashion, to bring into the Church of *England*, their pretended

Disci-

Booke. 3. *English Scottizing for Discipline by Practice.* 95

Disciplinarian government, of themselves, and by their owne authority, without any further staying (as they had done) for the civill Magistrate, albeit they pretend now the contrary: then it is fit that I produce some further matter to this purpose.

Amongst sundry things in the said booke of *Discipline*, let these few be well considered of, & weighed. It is there sayd, *Presbyterium in singulis Ecclesiis constituendum est*, there ought to be erected in every Church a Presbytery. Now if they had meant, (as it is pretended) not to have put their book, or at the least some chiefe parts thereof in practice, untill it should have been established by *Act* of *Parliament*, they would have sayd for *constituendum est*, there ought to bee erected, *constituatur*, let there be erected in every parish a Presbytery.

Againe, in all these assemblies prescribed in the booke, this was one point to be still inquired of: *utrum disciplina vigeat*, whether the Discipline had any life in it, or were esteemed, or continued: which question had beene frivolous, and very unmeet to have beene continued, as prescribed by Law, if the discipline it selfe had beene allowed by *Act* of *Parliament*, before that question should have beene moved. *Cap. de convent. ecclesiæ.*

Furthermore saith the booke: *in funeribus desuescendum est commodè, ab habendis concionibus, quod periculum sit ne superstitionem quorundam foveant, aut vanitati inserviant:* The Preachers *must leave off by little and little, as they may conveniently, to preach at burials, least thereby they nourish the superstition of some men, or give over themselves to the preservation of vanity*, *Cap. de concionibus ad ecclesiam habendis.*

Likewise, *festi dies sunt commodè abolendi:* holy daies (as we tearme them) *must be abolished*, *commodè, as they may, handsomely.* Now, if this booke had not beene meant, to have

have beene put in practice in these two points, before it had come forth, authorised by law: they would have said for the reasons alledged: *from henceforth let there be, or it is ordered, that there shall be no more preaching at burials, nor holy dayes observed, or let them henceforth be abolished.*

Moreover: *reliquæ liturgiæ tota ratio in sacramentorum administratione, & ex usu ecclesiæ in nuptiarum benedictione consistit. Cujus forma commodissima est, quæ ab ecclesiis usurpatur, quæ Disciplinam ex Dei verbo instaurârunt.* The rest of the liturgy doth consist in the administration of the Sacraments, and (as the use of the Church is,) in blessing of mariages. The forme whereof, is most fit and commodious, that is used by those Churches, which have erected the discipline, according to the word of God.

Cap. de reliqu. Liturg. officiis.

In the *Parliament* (27. of her Majestie: as I remember) the brethren having made another booke, tearmed at that time: *A booke of the forme of common prayers, &c.* and contayning in it the effect of their whole pretended discipline: the same booke was penned, altogether statute and law-like, and their petition in the behalfe of it was: vz. *May it therefore please your maiesty, &c. that it may be enacted, &c. that the booke hereunto annexed, &c. intituled: a booke of the forme of common prayers, administration of Sacraments, &c. and every thing therein contained, may be from henceforth authorized, put in ure, & practised throughout all your maiesties dominions.* Se here, when they hoped to have attained to their purposes by law, and to have had the same accordingly established: they offered to the *Parliament* a booke of their owne, for the *forme* of *common prayers, &c.* and thought it (as it seemeth) altogether inconvenient, to leave every minister to his owne choyce, to use what forme hee list, other then such as were allowed in some Church, which had received the Discipline: for any such they liked of indefinitly.

Whereby

Whereby to me it seemeth manifest, that they never meant, to have required the enacting of that Chapter, *de reliquis liturgiæ officiis*, but onely to set downe, what course their brethren should follow for the *interim*, untill they might take further order for a booke of their owne.

Lastly, in all this whole booke of *Discipline*, there is not once mention made of any authority, or office, in or over the Church, belonging to the Christian *civill* Magistrate. Hee hath not so much, as either voyce or place, in any of their *Synods*, as a member thereof, except he be chosen to be an *Elder*. Hee hath not any power assigned unto him to call a *Synod* : no, though it bee a *Nationall Synod* : nor so much as to appoint the particular times or places of their meetings, nor (which is most strange,) so much as that his assent, is to bee required to any of their Canons. But all these things are set downe in this booke, as of right to appertaine unto their Ministers and Elders. For the tryall whereof, I must needs referre you to the booke it selfe, (which is in many mens hands,) where you shall finde the brethren ascribe that to themselves, which in the greatest darknesse of Popery, all the BBs. in the Land (for ought I doe remember) durst never challenge. Which is a proofe sufficient, that either they meant by cunning to have deprived her Majesty, by her owne consent, of all her *regall* authority, in these, and such like causes of the Church, as not of right belonging unto her (which they will not acknowledge)or otherwise, that they had agreed without her consent, to take this authority unto themselves: which(if they had any conscience) they would not stick to confesse; that being assuredly their currant doctrine, as in some other place it shall hereafter more fully appeare.

But it may be said that these are onely collections. Well, let them bee, as they are. Indeed there is no cause, why I

O should

should stand upon collections, having yet in store most evident demonstrations.

Chap. XI.
Further proofe for their practise of their Discipline out of the articles they subscribed.

There hath beene often mention made, of the articles, whereunto the brethren subscribed, for their allowance and practise of the said booke of *Discipline*: and they are word for word, as here I doe set them downe, according to the deposition of those, that subscribed unto them, and as they are to bee shewed under Maister *Wights* hand.

We the brethren assembled together, in the name of God, having heard and examined, by the word of God, according to our best abilitie and judgement in it, a draught of discipline essentiall, and necessary for all times, and Synodicall, gathered out of the Synods, and use of the Churches; have thought good to testifie, concerning it as followeth.

We acknowledge and confesse the same, agreeable to Gods most holy word, so farre as we are able to judge or discerne of it, excepting some few points, which we have sent to our Reverend brethren of this Assembly, for their further resolution.

We affirme it to be the same, which we desire to be established in this Church, by daily praier to God: which we promise (as God shall offer opportunity, and give us to discerne it so expedient) by humble suit unto her Maiesties honourable Councel, and the Parliament, and by all other lawfull and convenient meanes, to further and advance, so far as the lawes, and peace, and the present estate of our Church will suffer it, and not enforce to the contrary.

Wee

We promise to guid our selves, and to be guided by it; and according to it.

For more especiall declaration of some points more important and necessarie, we promise uniformely, to follow such order, when we preach the word of God, as in the booke by us is set downe, in the Chapters *of the office of Ministers of the word, of preaching or sermons, of Sacraments, of Baptisme, and of the Lords supper.*

Further also, wee promise to follow the order set downe in the Chapters *of the meetings, as farre as it concerneth the Ministers of the word. For which purpose, wee promise to meet every sixe weekes together, in* Classical *conferences, with such of the brethren here assembled, as for their neighbourhood may fit us best; and such other, as by their advise we shall bee desired to joyne with us.*

The like wee promise, for Provinciall *meetings every halfe yeere from our conferences, to send unto them, as is set downe in the* Chapter, *concerning the* Provinces, *and the conferences belonging unto them, beeing divided according to the order following.*

Likewise also, that we will attend the general assembly *everie yeere, and at all* Parliaments, *and as often as by order it shall be thought good, to be assembled.* Hitherto the Articles.

Now by these Articles, and by their subscription unto them, it is most evident, that the pretences made by some, are but meerly shiftes: as that their purpose onely was, to have the booke in readinesse against a *Parliament*, and that they subscribed the Articles to no other end, but onely to testifie their agreement in iudgement, for that they were charged to disagree amongst themselves. For if that had beene their intent, it had beene sufficiently performed, by subscribing to the first Article onely. But they proceede on further, and entered into a certaine *league*, or *association*, binding themselves by promise, under their hands, what they

(for

(for their owne parts) will attempt, and as they might performe.

In the second Article, (as it is apparent,) there are other lawfull meanes promised to bee undertaken, (for the advancing of the *Discipline*,) then *prayers* to God, and *supplications* to her Majesty and the Parliament. Whereupon *Maister Littleton* (a subscriber) being examined, what hee understood *those meanes to bee*, answereth upon his oath, *that hee thinketh their private conferences, were meant to bee those lawfull meanes mentioned in the Article*. Which is according to the resolution of the brethren in *London*, set downe before, out of *Maister Edmonds* examination: viz. *that seeing they could not prevaile by suite to the State, the Ministers themselves should set up* the Discipline, *as they should be able*. And *Maister Johnson*, is also as direct upon his oath, to the same effect, saying:

Littleton.
Before the Commissioners.

Before the Commissioners.

It was a generall conclusion amongst all the Classes, *and brethren, that forasmuch as the* Discipline *required by petitions, could not be publikely established by law, it was thought in conscience necessary to establish it, and practise it privatly, to which purpose also, every man was to use his endeavour, to encrease the number of such, as would conforme themselves that way.*

Againe it is promised in the same *Article*, that they would proceed with their said meanes, for the advancement of their *Discipline, so far as the peace of the present state of our Church would suffer*.

Now how farre that is, it hath beene before touched in the *decrees* of one of their *Synods*, 1583. for (as men most strangely bewitched) they imagined, that they could so cunningly play their feats, as that they might (in effect) set up their own *Discipline*, secretly, under hand, and yet never disturbe the present government of the Church.

For as peace is here taken in their sense, one King or governe-

governement may invade another, with all kinde of hostility, and say (as they doe) that they meane but peace. The truth is, they may have peace in their mouths, but in their actions, there is nothing lesse. So as this their restraint (being but a vaine pretence) doth no way indeed impeach my assertion.

Furthermore, whereas also it followeth in the same Article, (*and not enforce to the contrarie,*) Maister *Littleton* being examined upon his oath *what that should meane*: answereth that he *himselfe, Maister Snape, Maister Proudloe, and others, did agree to put the said Articles and Discipline in execution and practise so far as the peace and the present estate of the Church will suffer, and not enforce to the contrary. That is to say: till the Magistrate did enjoyne them or enforce them, to leave the practise of the said* Discipline: and in another place, *till the Magistrate did inhibite them to the contrary, and force them to leave it.* And further, hee also saith: *that they did agree to guide themselves by the said booke of Discipline, and according to it, with the same limitation.* Now what if by their secret practises, (to draw away the peoples hearts from the present government of the Church) they could have procured such strength and number, to have followed them, as that no reasonable restraint, or force of the Magistrate had bin able to have encountered and suppressed them? I doe but aske the question.

In the Starre Chamber.

In the rest of the *Articles* there are but two generall points: the one contained in the third *Article*, concerning the uniformity, which they promise to use in their Ministery: and the other is, as touching their agreement, to follow the orders set downe for their meetings: *Classicall*, contained in the fourth: *Provinciall*, in the fift: *Nationall*, in the sixt Article.

So as where before in the second *Article*, they had mentioned

tioned *other meanes*, whereby they had promised to advance their *Discipline*, besides *praiers to God*, and *supplications to her Majestie*: they doe now in part explaine themselves, in the other *Article* following, and doe set downe, what *meanes* they that were Ministers would use and put in practise, for the advancement of it, viz. the two points mentioned, that is, their *uniformity in preachings*, and their *meetings*: according to Maister *Littletons* deposition, in these words: *they meant by those meanes, in the second Article, their conferences: as he thinketh.* But to carry this matter past thinking, let Maister *Fen* be heard, who saith: *that hee agreed to put some things of the booke in execution, according to the subscription*: let Maister *Lord* be heard, who saith: *that hee agreed to put some things of the said booke in practise, as in the Articles is contained.* But let their *Coryphæus* Maister *Cartwright* himselfe be heard, who saith: *that he agreed to put two points of the Articles in execution: viz. touching the order of preaching, and touching the assemblies.*

Chap. XII.

It is confessed that they agreed to put one point of their booke in practise without her Majesties assent: what it is: and of strange names given to children.

Now because it appeareth, in the third, fourth, fift and sixth of the said *Articles*, that concerning both these points, they referre themselves to certain *Chapters* of their book of *Discipline*, I have thought it very convenient, to set down, out of the said *Chapters*, some of those particulars, which by their said subscription they bound themselves to practise, without any farther staying for the civill Magistrate: and withal to adioyne some part of their constancie, (if so I may

abuse

abuse a good word,) in the perfourming of their promises, touching the said particulars. Maister *Littleton* beeing sworne, dealeth (as it seemeth) very directly to this purpose: for (as hee saith) concerning the contents of the foure last *Articles*, hee for his part, whilest hee was of that company, perfourmed his promise, and (he thinketh) that the rest that subscribed did the like. But to the particulars: and first of the first point. Exam. before the Commi.

The Minister, that is to preach, shall appoint the Psalme that is to be sung, &c. After the Psalme, let there be made a short admonition to the congregation, how they shall prepare themselves rightly to pray. Let a Prayer follow, containing the confession of sinnes, &c. and concluded with the Lords Prayer. After the Sermon, let Prayers bee made for grace, that the auditers may profit by the doctrine delivered: also for the whole Church, and all particular callings: and let them end likewise with the Lords Prayer. Then a Psalme, &c. and lastly let the conclusion bee made, with some short forme of blessing the congregation, taken out of the Scriptures. De officio Minist. &c.

For the practise of this order: I referre the proofe of it to all those, who have observed the manner of any of the brethrens behaviour, in their severall Churches. The most of them, that are but Doctors, (as they terme themselves) and readers of Lectures in other mens charges, doe seldome or never come to the service, which is read in the Church according to her Majesties Lawes: but under pretence of studying for their Sermons, doe absent themselves, untill service be done, or at the least almost finished, and then they come in, (gravely I warrant you,) and doe goe to this their owne forme of service.

The rest of the fraternity, that have cures of their owne, some of them will have a *Parliament Minister*, (as they terme him) under them, to say service: and then hee himselfe

104 *English Scottizing, for discipline by Practise.* Book 1.

selfe dealeth, as it hath beene noted of the Doctor: but others, that are not able to have such a one, they for their *safer standing* (as their terme is) doe use some piece of our service booke, and peradventure read a lesson, (which things they affirme, as it hath beene touched, may bee performed as well by those that are not Ministers, as by them.) And then they in like sort, doe begin their owne ministeriall function, and proceed according to the foresaid fashion, subscribed unto, and promised.

But to proceed unto their practice of other points of that booke.

<small>De concionibus habendis, &c.</small> *The Preachers must leave off, by little and little, as they may conveniently, to preach at burials: least thereby they nourish the superstition of some men, or give over themselves to the preservation of vanity.*

<small>De Baptismo.</small> *Let not women onely offer infants to Baptisme, but the father, if it may be conveniently, or els some others in his name.*

Let perswasions be used, that such names as doe savour either of Paganisme or Popery, be not given to children at their Baptisme, but principally those, whereof there are examples in the Scriptures.

Whether these points, (especially for two of them) have beene practised by the brethren or not, the *new Church-yard* in *London*, and many brables in the country, about urging of the naturall fathers to become Godfathers to their owne Children, &c. can more then sufficiently witnesse. And for the third, it is also sundry wayes apparent. <small>Penner. Barbon. Aire. Wigginton. &c. before the Commissioners.</small> For whence else doe these new names and fancies proceed? *The Lord is neare. More tryall. Reformation. Discipline. Joy againe. Sufficient. From-above. Free-gifts. More-fruit. Dust,* and many other such like. But *Richard Hangar* of *Northampton*, did first under his hand, and after upon his oath, deliver an especiall history (to this purpose) of

Book 3. *English Scottizing for Discipline by Practise.* 105
of giving names.

Snape *would not Baptise one* Christopher Hodgkinsons *childe, because hee would have the childe called* Richard. *The order was this,* Hodgkinson *obtained promise of* Snape, *that he would christen his childe: But (saith* Snape *you must then give it a Christian name, allowed in the Scriptures. The party told him, that his wives father, whose name was* Richard, *desired the name. Well (saith* Snape *) you must doe as I bid you, that when you come, the congregation be not troubled. But notwithstanding, the said* Hodgkinson *not thinking it would have been made a matter of such importance, the childe was brought.* Snape *proceeded in the action: till he came to the naming of the child. And when he heard, that they called the child* Richard, *and that they would give him no other name; he staied there, and would not in any wise Baptize the child. And so the child was carried away thence, and was Baptized the weeke following, at* Alhallowes, *being named* Richard.

Of likelyhood, the brethren have found this thing to be a matter of great importance: that they will rather leave an infant unbaptized, then give him such a name.

Chap. XIII.

A second point of their Booke confessed to bee agreed upon, for the practise of it, without her Majesties assent.

Now I will come to Master *Cartwrights* second point, that is of the *meetings*: and set downe the Chapters, whereunto in the *Articles* subscribed, they referred themselves; that thereby hereafter no man, that will read them, may doubt of their purpose, of not staying for the Magistrate: which are as follow, so neere as
P   I could

I could by translation of them out of Latine, expresse their meaning.

Of the Assembly of the Church.

Mutuall conference is to be practised in the Church by common Assemblies, but in these, matters Ecclesiasticall are to bee handled; and such chiefly as concerne those Churches, wherof the Assembly doth consist.

They shall not determine, (except they be requested,) of any thing touching other Churches: but shall onely decree, that such matter is to be referred to the next greater Assembly: Let the matters and order of things to be handled in them be thus.

Next after the view or calling of those that be present, (wherin withall the names of such as be absent must bee noted, that in the next Assembly, they may either yeeld sufficient reason of their absence, or else be censured, by the judgement of the Assembly,) first let the Acts of the next Assembly afore, (that was of the same sort) bee read: to the intent, that if any thing of them were left then undone, it may be dispatched. Then, let those matters bee done, that are peculiar to the Assembly in hand. And first, let every of them deliver the instructions from their Churches, in the same order that they sit, together with the Fiduciary or Letters of credence of the Churches: next, let there bee * censures had of the Churches of that Assembly: whereby may bee understood how they are framed and used: whether the Doctrine and the Discipline have their course in them, and whether the officers of them doe that which appertaineth, and such like.

or inquisition (as I take the meaning.

Besides let them decree those things that shall concerne either the common behoofe of all the Churches of that Assembly, or of any one of them: and this course will be sufficient enough, for the view and oversight of the Churches.

Lastly, (if it so seeme good) let there by inquiry and Censures had even of those, which be delegated to meet in that Assembly.

Such as are to meet in the Assemblies, let them be chosen by the Suffrages of those Churches or Assemblies, that have interest

or

or to doe in it: and out of these, let such onely be chosen, as have exercised the publike office in that Church, either of a Minister, or of an Elder; and which have subscribed both to the doctrine and Discipline, and which have undertaken to behave themselves in all things according to the word of God.

It shal be lawful for other Elders & Ministers, yea and for Deacons and students in Divinity, by the appointment of the Assembly, (especially if they be such as doe exercise themselves in interpreting the Scriptures in the Assembly,) to be both present, and to be asked their judgements: these of the latter sort are therefore to be admitted, that their judgements to handle the affaires of the Church, may hereby both be tryed and sharpned. Yet let none be counted to have a voyce, but those onely, that were chosen by the Church, and which bring their commissions consigned unto them.

If any matter be to bee consulted of, that is of speciall importance, let the President of the last superior Assembly, or the Minister of that Church, in which the next Assembly is to be made, send it over in due time unto the Ministers of all the Churches of that Assembly; to the intent they may afore treate thereof, with those of their charge, and so may know and report their judgements. In making choice of a place for the Assemblies, respect is to be had of neernesse, and other opportunities: in case any party may justly find himselfe grieved above the rest.

It is expedient, that in every Ecclesiasticall Assembly, there be a President, which may governe the Assembly, and that he be from time to time chaunged, if it may bee conveniently; and hee must be thus chosen, viz.

He that was President of the last Assembly of that kind afore, or the Minister of that congregation, where the Assembly is made (conceiving first a prayer directed to that purpose) shall preferre unto the Assembly, the motion for choice of a President.

The President being thus chosen, (conceiving first a Prayer fitting unto the whole action and Assembly,) shall call over the names of those, which be present and which be absent, and note them: that the absents may be called upon at the next Assembly, to yeeld a reason of their absence.

Which if it be not sufficient, let them be censured, by the authority of the Assembly. Then let him read the Acts of the last Assembly, that if any thing thereof remaine, it may then bee dispatched. Then shall he aske of every one in order as they sit, their letters fiduciarie or of credence, and their instructions signed. Which being propounded in the same order, and sufficiently debated by all their opinions, he shall ask their judgements, and gather the suffrages, and pronounce what the greater part adjudgeth. Which he shall procure to be put into Acts, that the Delegates of the severall Churches, may procure copies and transcripts to be made, which they may impart unto those Churches, to whom it appertaineth.

The President also, by the judgement and authority of the assembly, is to give answer, either by word of mouth, or by letters, to such as require it. If any censures be to be inflicted, he is to performe them. He shall also take care, that all things be godly and quietly carried, by exhorting them unto quietnes, and moderation of minde, one bearing with another, as need shall bee, and by preferring up, such as be wilfull and contentious, unto the Assembly: lastly he shall propound unto them, touching the time of their next meeting: and then with exhortation unto them, chearefully to go forward in their duty, and with thanksgiving, he shall curteously dismisse them.

Before the dismission of the Assembly, let no man depart but with leave.

The Assemblies according to their severall kinds, if they bee greater, are of more; if they be lesse, they are of lesse authority. Therefore it is lawfull to appeale from a lesse Assembly to a greater,

ter, if any man think he have injury, except the fact be most evident and plaine unto every man: but yet none otherwise, but that the judgement of the Assembly shall hold, untill it shall be otherwise adjudged, in an Assembly of greater authority.

Assemblies are either { Classes. or Synods.

Classes are conferences of the fewest Ministers of Churches, standing neare together, as for example of twelve.

The chosen men of all the severall Churches of that Assembly, are to meet in conference; that is to say, for every Church a Minister and an Elder: and they shall meete every fortnight. They shall chiefly endeavour the oversight and censure of that Classis: searching particularly, whether in them every thing be done according to the holy doctrine and discipline of the Gospel: viz. Whether any question bee arisen, touching any point of Doctrine.

Whether the Ecclesiasticall discipline have his course.

Whether any Minister be wanting in any of the Churches, that they may speedily provide a fit person.

Whether the rest of the Elders and Officers of the Church be appointed in every Church.

Whether care be had, over schollers, and the poore.

In what points the Classes doe want advice, for the further advancing of the Gospel among them.

Before they make an end, let some of the Ministers present, make a sermon, either in course, or being chosen therto by voyces: of whom the rest of the Ministers (secluding the Elders) shall judge among themselves: and if in any point, it shall be requisite, they shal monish him brotherly; weighing every thing, according to the course afore laid-downe in the Chapter touching those things

things, which are to be performed by him that preacheth to the congregation.

Synods.

A Synod is an Assembly of chosen men, from more Churches, then those that be in one Classis or conference.

In these, the Articles of the holy Discipline and Synodicall, must alwaies be read: also in them, (after all other things be finished,) censures or inquisition made, upon all that be present: and the supper of the Lord shall bee celebrated by them, in and with that congregation, where the Assembly is made, if conveniently it may be.

Of Synods there be two sorts: the first is particular, and this conteineth under it

both { Provinciall and Nationall } Synods:

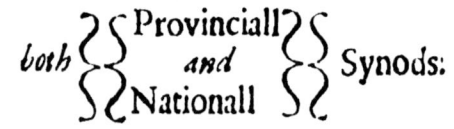

A Provinciall Synod, is an Assembly of those, which be delegated from all the Classes or conferences of that Province.

Let every province containe in it 24. Classes.

This may be a fit order, for the Assembling together of a Synod Provinciall. viz. Let this care be laid upon some certaine Church, by consent of the Synod: let that Church, with advise of the Classis whereof it is, prefixe the place and time for the Assembly: let other Churches, send unto such Church, those matters which seeme unto them of some difficultie to determine; and likewise those matters, that doe appertaine to the whole Province, and that diligently in convenient season: to th'intent, that that Church may in due time give advertisement unto all the Classes of the Province, both of the time and place, and of the matters to be handled: so that such as are sent, may come better prepared and that they may judge thereof, according to the resolution of

their

Book 3. *English Scottizing, for Discipline by Practise.* 111
their owne severall Classes or conferences.

Let every Classis send unto the Provinciall Synod two Ministers, and as many Elders.

It shall bee called every halfe yeare, or more often, untill the Discipline be confirmed.

But before a Nationall Synod be celebrated, let it be called three moneths afore, that they may prepare, and furnish up those things, that belong unto it.

Let the Acts of all the Provinciall Synods bee sent unto the Nationall, by that Church, in which the Provinciall Assembly was had, and let every Minister be furnished, with the copies of the Acts, and with the reasons used.

The Nationall is a Synod consisting of the Delegats from all the Synods Provinciall, that are within the dominion of one common-wealth. Let the manner of calling it be the same that is appointed for calling the Provinciall, except the Synod it selfe shall take other order herein: viz. by some certaine Church: yet so, as the said Church doe appoint for place and time (to hold in it) such as the Provinciall Synod of that Church, which shall next ensue, shall determine, and thinke good.

For the Nationall Synod, three Ministers and three Elders must be chosen, out of every Synod Provinciall.

In it the common affaires of all the Churches of the whole nation and kingdome, are to be handled: as of Doctrine, Discipline, and ceremonies: causes not decided in inferiour Assemblies, Appellations, and such like.

By the decree of the Nationall Synod, one is to bee chosen, which shall reduce the Commentaries or Acts of all the severall Churches, into one body.

Hitherto concerning particular Assemblies. Now followes the universall or œcumenicall Synod of the whole world.

And

And this is the Synod, that confifteth and is gathered together, of the chofen men out of every particular Nationall Synod.

The Acts of all Synods are to be reduced into one body.

And thus farre thefe Chapters of the *meetings*; the particular points whereof, Maifter *Cartwright* and his companions have bound themfelves, by their fubfcriptions, to put in practife, without any further expectation for her Majefties affent. And according to thefe points, (as their numbers and opportunities have ferved their turns) they have accomplifhed their bonds and promifes; as by that which hath been faid, and by depofitions upon oathes, concerning their meetings and dealings in them, is moft apparent, to any that is not blinded with wilfull obftinacy.

Chap. XIIII.

Moe points of their booke put in practife, fafts, calling of Minifters, presbyteries, cenfure, &c.

Furthermore alfo, they have not contented themfelves with the execution of thefe things onely, but they have befides proceeded, in like manner, with the full practifing almoft of all the reft of the booke.

It is moft notorious, that according to the Doctrine thereof, they have taken upon them, to appoint publicke Fafts: and then efpecially they have done it, when their fellowes have beene moft bufie, to trouble the prefent eftate of the Church. Befides that, thefe Fafts with their feverall fermons and other prophecyings,

Book 3. *English Scottizing, for Discipline by Practise.* 113

ings, have had another principall use, viz. (as *Lord* did write to *Fen* of Maister *Cartwrights* pleasure) that the day following, the brethren might talke of other matters.

Likewise (saith Maister *Johnson*) touching the election and making of Ministers, I thinke they observe, asmuch as they can, the order prescribed in the said book of *Discipline*. As about Proudloe of Weedenbeck his admission, (as I have heard) and Snapes and Larkes. The manner whereof is, that they renounce the calling, they have had of the Bishops: and doe take it againe, from the approbation of the Classis. And againe, they will be content to accept orders from the Bishop, as a civil matter, but doe not thereby account themselves Ministers, untill the godly brethren of some Classes have allowed them. But more fully Richard Hawgar, The first degree they have entered into, is this, that teaching all Ministers, which are called according to the order of the Church of England, to bee unlawfull: they doe urge such as they dare trust (and who are Ministers already) to seeke at their Classis a new approbation, which they terme the Lords ordinance. *(Iohnson before the Commissioners.)* *(Ri. Hawgar his deposition.)*

In this action, the Minister before allowed of, must renounce his former calling, and take that calling, (whereby hee must stand) of them.

The manner whereof, is this: When any doe yeeld hereunto, they appoint a day of their Classis, &c. As the example following will shew. One master Hocknel, being to have a benefice, was willed (by his Patron) to bring some testimoniall, of the Ministers of the shire, for his good conversation. Whereupon hee came to Maister Snape. who dealt with him (as is afore mentioned,) and Hocknell having beene a Minister before, (some six or seaven yeares) yeelding: Snape, with his companions gave him a text, and appointed him a day.

Q   A1

English Scottizing, for Discipline by Practise. Book 3.

At which time the Classis met in Saint Peters, and he preached. After, they assembled themselves, willing Hocknell to stand aloofe. Then Maister Penry beganne to make a speech, exhorting them to be carefull, to call upon God: to deale without affection in this their action, &c. After which, they fel to the matter. Some liked that the man should be admitted, and some otherwise. Those that were against him made these two reasons: First, that hee had not jumped meete, in delivering the Metaphore, which was in his text: Secondly, because he was neither Grecian nor Hebrician. So as they over-ruling the rest, Hocknell was called for, and in some sort commended: but yet the Speaker of the Classis told him, he must take more paines at his book, before they could allow of him as a fit Minister. Hereupon Maister Hocknell and they fell out, and he (contemning their censure) did proceed and tooke possession of his benefice.

When they call a man that is not already a Minister, then having used the order before mentioned, they command him to goe to the Bishops, as to a civill Magistrate, for his writings, (which they terme by a prettie name that this ex. hath forgotten:) and this they say, is onely for his safe standing in his former calling received of them: not that thereby hee receiveth any power to be a Minister. On this sort was Maister Lark (dwelling a little from Wellingborow) called.

After this calling by them, the parties so called may preach here and there, as he thinketh good, until he be called to a charge, and then he must go to the Bishop, for his better standing, and so the people calling him, he is a full Minister.

Maister Snape being a Minister already, renounced that his first calling; was called by the Classis: by that calling hee preached, but would not administer the Lords Supper: After the parrish of Saint Peters, knowing that he must not account himselfe

Book 3. *English Scottizing, for Discipline by Practise.* 115

a full Minister, untill some particular congregation, had chosen him, they chose him for their Minister, and so he standeth at this present. Thus farre *Hawgar*.

It is likewise deposed by two, that Maister *Snape*, for the answering of a question propounded unto him, said, *that rather then he would have stood by vertue of any Letters of orders, he would have beene hanged upon the gallowes.* Ri. Holmen Richard Hawgar before the Commissioners.

But let Maister *Snape* speake himselfe: *Touching the substance of my calling to the Ministerie, I affirme that I had it of the Church of God, being approved by the learned and godly neighbour Ministers, and chosen by the people of my charge, to that function. Touching that allowance that I had of the Bishop, I take it to be a thing meerly civill, belonging to a civill Magistrate, which authority he hath by Act of Parliament: and which therfore I might lawfully receive at his hands, for the peaceable execution of my Ministery.* Snape, in a writing of his owne hand.

Againe, concerning the *Presbyteries*, (which the booke affirmeth should be in every parish:) they want (in effect) nothing of all their whole platforme, if they could but once attaine unto the publike erecting up of those *thrones*. And how farre it is likely they have already prevailed therin, without staying any longer for her majesty; let these things following, whereof some have beene touched already, make it known unto you. mention hath beene made of a *Presbyterie* set up at *Wandesworth*. It was a decree of the London brethren, *that the Ministers should by little and little, as much as possibly they might, draw the Discipline into practise, though they concealed the names, either of Presbytery, Elder or Deacon, making little account of the names for the time, so their offices might secretly bee established.* There was an order set downe in an Assembly (1583. as I take it) *for the converting of Churchwardens and Collectors into Elders* M. Edmonds

Q 2   ders

116 *English Scottizing, for Discipline by Practise.* Book 3.

ders and Deacons: as before in the Actes themselves it appeareth. According to this order the brethren afterward sent their directions abroad, to their fellowes, for their execution of it. *I received* (saith Maister *Barbon*) *from our faithfull brother Maister Gellibrand, a direction of the brethren, concerning the converting of Churchwardens into Elders, and Collectors into Deacons.* Richard Holmes affirmeth that *by such speeches as he hath heard, hee doth verily thinke, that the Ministers in their Classes have resolved to erect up their severall Presbyteries in their owne parishes:* With him agreeth Maister *Johnson, according to the rules of that booke, I thinke that secretly in most places, where the brethren of the Classes are, there are Elders chosen, and that they put the Discipline in practise, so farre as they may, amongst themselves, without any apparent shew thereof, to the overthrow of their safe-standing.* Further also he deposeth, that *he himselfe hath beene blamed divers times privately, in that hee would make no such choice of Elders, (where he preached,) to practise the Discipline.* And what els should *Gellibrand* meane, by these words in a Letter to *Field? I have written to Maister Cartwright severally, and jointly to him and the Elders, signifying my readines, and what adversaries there are.*

 Lastly there was a nomination of Elders, at *Kilsby* in *Northampton-shire*, made by Maister *Lee* the pastor, in the yeare 1588. Their names as it was deposed before Sir *George Farmer* and Sir *John Spencer*, were, *William Greene, Roger Cowley, Thomas Hall, Richard Wolfe, John Browne,* and *William Mariat: which six* (saith the deponent,) Maister *Lee* thought sufficient to determine and end al matters of controversie in the said towne. Henry Pinton *also affirmeth, that hee being enformed of this election of Elders by the said* Browne *and others, would not yeeld his consent thereunto, but said he would stand to the lawes of this realme, appointed by her Majestie.*

One

[margin: Barbon to Field. Holmes. Johnson. Ioh. Browne]

Book 3. *English Scottizing, for Discipline by Practise.*

One especial reason, (as it was enformed) why *Pinson* refused in this sort to joyne with his neighbours, was, for that there should have bin some punishment, inflicted by the said Elders upon his sonne, for flinging a stone at *Elder-Mariats* window, which he would none of, but was faine to fly to her Majesties lawes.

So here then it appeareth (in some sort,) whether the brethren mean to stay any more for the civill Magistrate, in erecting of their *Presbyteries*, then they confesse they did, concerning their *uniformity* in Sermons and tripartite *meetings*.

Besides, it doth also appertaine to the further proofe of the said *Presbyteries*, that (as it seemeth) some of those censures have beene used: for example, *excommunication:* Which (by the rules of the Discipline booke) are of right to bee exercised by them. One *Bluet* a Minister (as I suppose) being excommunicated (as it seemeth) did write a Letter to *Field* and *Egerton:* wherein hee is most earnest, that upon his repentance hee might bee restored againe to the Church. *Woe is me* (saith he) *that I am cast out of your presence this day: but shame and sorrow is unto the cause. And if this woe and shame did but touch the body, it were tolerable: for then at the day of death I should end my misery, and no more heare the words of reproach. For now every one that seeth me, reproveth me: and I am become a rebuke unto all men. But this is not all: woe is me, that there is a partition-wall, betweene heaven and my conscience, &c. If my offence may not bee passed by, without further confession: even before God and his Church in London, will I lye down and licke the dust at your feet, and confesse more against my selfe then any of you know.* Severe *Catoes*, I warrant you. But is this the matter they contend for, that men may fall downe, and kisse their feet?

There is also another example to this effect, worthy of

Q 3 your

your remembrance: one *La. Thomson* writeth in this sort of it: *I thinke of him as an unsound member, unfit to bee continued in the body, unles he would be subject to the government of a body, especially the body of our saving God.* The partie meant by *Thomson*, was (as I take it) Maister *Wilcox*, the author of that *admonition*, which caused the first breaking-out of all those troubles that since have ensued. This appeareth by foure letters, written about the yeare 1 5 8 3. three of them from *Field* to *Wilcox*, and one from *Wilcox* to *Field*. What the cause was, though it bee expressed in one of the said Letters, I omit to rehearse it, no wayes minding to touch any mans private behaviour or infirmities. But this I must tell you, that the brethren, (that is in *Thomsons* sense, *the body of our saving God*,) were so displeased and angry with him, that they suspended him from his Ministerie, and did use their censure of *excommunication* against him.

If you aske me how *Wilcox* tooke this course at their hands, I answer, even as *Pinson* before named did, when his sonne should have beene punished: he disliked it so much, as that hee began to call their authority (for such kind of their proceedings,) in question, he refused to submit himselfe to their censures, and told *Field* plainly, *that he had bin dealt disorderly withall, both for matter and manner:* adding, *that he had perhaps concealed as great infirmities of* Fields, *and of some others, as his were*

With these and many such like words *Field* was greatly provoked, and for his owne part defied him. *whereas* (saith hee) *for the hiding of your owne shame, you beginne to score up my faults, which you say are six in number, as great as yours, if you should utter them: I say it is no help to you, but testifieth that old pride, hypocrisie and malice, which long time hath lurked in that cankered heart of yours, &c. But I doe defie you, &c.*

Book 3. *English Scottizing, for Discipline by Practise.* 119

&c. And for his refusing of their proceedings, *you ought not* (saith *Field*) *so lightly to esteeme, that holy censure of the brethren, but in true repentance to have hidden your face, &c.* Againe, *if God hath made you an instrument, to seeke for the advancement of Christs Scepter, kisse it your selfe and be subject unto it, &c.* Againe, *if you love Christ and his Church before your owne glory; and your owne sinnes have shut up your mouth, then bee silent for ever.* And notwithstanding that *Wilcox* took exception to their authority, yet in the Letter wherein *Field* answereth that point, and many others, he beginneth thus: *The Lord Jesus open your eyes, and give you such a true sense, and feeling of your sins, that howsoever you (for a time) be throwne to Sathan; in the end your soule may bee saved, and you may feele assurance of eternall life, &c.*

What the issue of this matter was amongst them, I finde it not. It seemeth that in the end, *Wilcox* for lacke of his former maintenance, (which was withheld from him by the brethrens procurement, and upon perswasion that after a time hee should be restored to his Ministery againe, and in the meane space bee relieved) was faine to yeeld and to submit himselfe unto their censure, (by them termed *the Scepter of Christ.*) Marrie still he thought himselfe to be hardly used, and after some time of expectation, desired (as it seemeth) to know, how long he should undergoe their heavie indignation. Whereunto *Field* answered thus: *The brethren thought meet to admonish you, utterly to surcease: For how long or how short, mee thinks you should not enquire, considering the circumstances; who know very well your selfe, that if another were in your case, that no time can be limited. Neverthelesse, if you doubt the judgements to be too hard, that already is given, you may aske the private opinions of others your best friends, as of Maister* Cartwright, *and M.* Thomson, *who are of mind that you are for ever disabled to that function, &c.*

CHAP. XV.

Chap. XV.

They have joyned themselves into an association or brotherhood, and doe appropriate to their meetings, the name of the Church.

Here is often mention made, in the premisses of the brethren, but yet in none other sense, then they appropriate to themselves, in sundry of their writings and Letters, as, [a] *Salute the brethren, Salute the* [b] *reverend brethren, Maſter Travers, Chark, Barber, Gardner, Egerton. Salute* [c] *our moſt reverend brother Maiſter Cartwright. Salute* [d] *our reverend brother Maiſter Cartwright, and the reſt of the brethren. The* [e] *brethren ſalute you. Commend* [f] *me to all our brethren. Commend me* [g] *to all the brethren with you: the brethren with us here, are in health. Commend* [h] *me to Maiſter Chark and Maiſter Travers, with all the reſt of the brethren. Remember* [i] *me to the brethren. Let him* [k] *be accounted among the brethren, as he deſerveth. I writ to my Mother, to ſpeake to you and our good brethren, to provide me of ſome honeſt brother, to Catechiſe my family. To* [l] *Maiſter Field, with the reſt of the godly Miniſters, his brethren, in London. To his beloved* [m] *brother, Maiſter Field, and to all other his faithfull brethren, namely of the Miniſtery, at or about London. Our* [n] *brethren have determined. I truſt* [o] *you are ſo linked together, by the bond of brotherly love, and the deſire of the pure Diſcipline of the church, that nothing may ſunder you: the brethren aſſembled: the godly brethren: our poore brethren here,* [p] *at Oxford, do long to heare from you: and, in the Articles wherunto they ſubſcribed: we the brethren, &c.*

Upon the occaſion of theſe termes, and many other
ſuch

[Marginal notes:]
a Barbon to Field
Pig. to Field.
Snape to Stone.
b Barbon to Field.
c D. Chapman to Field
d Pig. to Field 1586.
e Gellibrand from Oxford to Field
f Wake to Field.
g Knewſtub to Field
h wade to Field.
i Barbon to Field.
k T. Thomſon to Field.
l Oxford to Field
m Wiggintō to Field
n D. Chapmā to Field.
o Gellibrand to Field.

Book 3. *English Scottizing, for Discipline by Practise.* 121

such like: it is found out by examination, that this *Classi-call* and reforming consort, with their followers, have divided themselves from all the rest of the ministery, and *Christi-ans* in *England*: and linked themselves into a new brotherhood, with this linke, viz. (*as Doctor Cricke termeth it*) *the desire of the pure Discipline*: thereby shewing themselves to be most notorious *Schismatickes*. Cricke to Field.

When *salutations are written*, (saith M^r. *Johnson*) *by the brethren that seeke reformation, as unto the godly brethren: the meaning is, (as I ever tooke it) to such as have submitted themselves unto the holy Discipline. Again, when the name Brother is given to Ministers, it signifieth them to be of some Classis, for their consulting and setting up of Christs kingdome: and when to the laitie, those that generally do joyne with the Ministers for the Discipline, and do every of them submit themselves to a Minister of some of the Classis, &c. And these, both Ministers and people are the godly brotherhood, denying the name properly of a godly brother or sister to any other.* The same also (in effect) hath he deposed in the *Starre-Chamber*: where he further addeth, *that thus he thought himselfe, when hee was of that brotherhood, and that it was so commonly maintained, both by him, and by the rest of the* Northampton Classis. Johnson.

And Master *Edmonds* in like manner, hath deposed as much to the same purpose, both in the *Starre-Chamber*, and before her Majesties *Commissioners for causes ecclesiasticall*: *This* (saith he) *I do know, that when salutations were sent, or letters written to* London *from some Ministers abroad, as from* Fen *or* Cartwright, *&c. to Maister* Field *and the rest, &c. thereby was alwayes meant properly the Ministers, or the brotherhood of the Ministery in* London: *and when they use the name or phrase of godly brethren, or sisters, or godly brotherhood or sisterhood, they meane generally both all the said Ministers, and likewise as many as do depend upon them for the cause of reformation. So* Edmonds

R   as

122 *English Scottizing, for Discipline by Practise.* Book 3.
as the rest of the Ministers and people, who and wheresoever, that doe not joyne with them, (as is before said) are altogether excluded out of their brotherhood: insomuch, as they will avoid the company of all other, as much as they can possibly, refusing either to buy or sell, or to eat or drinke with them.

Againe, it may not in any wise be omitted, that in their severall said letters and other writings, they use oftentimes the name of the *Church*, and of the *Churches*, in as lewd a sense, as they doe the name of brethren. Thus they write: *I know* [a] *the state of this Church: Make knowen to us the state of the Church with you. Our Churches* [b] *are in danger of such, as haveing beene of us, do renounce all fellowship with us.*

a Snape to Field.
b Knewstub to Field.

The [c] *hand of God is like to be heavy upon our Churches here, if the malice of Sathan, and his instruments be not prevented. A woman with us, &c. sometimes thought to be a friend to Religion, &c. giveth it forth, that Maister Walsh had laid witchcraft upon her. She would have had him convented by some of the Justices, but when he was once named she was repelled. Now she is come to London, &c. She deviseth new matter against him, and against us all, as that wee should have had meetings at her house, &c. And that we have a private jurisdictoin among our selves, thinking that this will make her entrance unto the Archbishop, or high Commissioners, &c. I pray you first conferre with Maister Walsh: and then deale, (as secretly as you may) to medicine these mischiefes.*

c Knewstub to Field.

Good Iustice.

It is long [d] *since I heard from you,* (saith one Blake) *of the state of the Church of* London. Another, *By M.* West [e] *& M.* Browne, *you shall understand the state of the Churches, wherein we are.* A third: *If my offence* [f] *may not be passed by without a further confession, even before God and his Church, in* London *will I lie downe, and licke the dust at your feete, and confesse, &c.* A fourth: *I received a letter* [g] *from you in the name of the rest of the brethren: whereby I understand your joyning together, in*

d Blake to Field.
e Gellibrand to Field.
f Rob Muet to Field and Egerton.
g Lenne to Fall.

chusing

Book 3.   *English Scottizing, for Discipline by Practise.*   123

chusing of my selfe, unto the Service of the Church, under the Earle of Leicester, *&c. I am ready to runne, if the Church command me, according to the holy decrees and orders of the Discipline.* By these their speeches it appeareth, that as they have cut off themselves from the fellowship of the rest of the *Christians* in *England*, by joyning themselves into a severall brotherhood: so have they already seduced her Majesties subjects, by gathering them together into a new societie, whereunto they doe appropriate the name of the Church: as though all other Churches in the Realme, were but as *Jewish Synagogues* or heathenish Assemblies. This is not, (you shall see) my bare collection: heare the witnesses, what they hereof have deposed.

In these brethrens speeches of the Church or Churches: it is to bee understood, that by the Church of England, *they meane the Church according to humane lawes and the Popes: which is ruled, (as they terme it) by an Antichristian government. And by the* Godly Churches, *or the* Churches of God *in England, they meane such places, congregations, or Assemblies, as doe embrace the reformation, and have such a Minister, as is of some* Classis. — Iohnson.

Sometime also by the Church, (as the Church of God in London) *is meant the Classis of the brethren, or their Synods. And so Maister* Edmonds: *when they use these, or the like speeches, in their writing or otherwise: viz. the Church or Churches of God here, wish this or that, or the Church in* London *hath done this or that: therby they especially mean the Ministers themselves.* — Edmonds.

But for the further clearing of this matter, because the chiefe *Rabbies* of this conspiracie, doe themselves preach in our materiall Churches, it is to be observed, that the parish where they preach, being assembled, is not the Church properly in their sense, but as many thereof onely, as are ioyned unto them with that inviolable bond mentioned:

viz. the

viz: the desire of the godly Discipline: and those furthermore, who leaving their owne *Parish Churches*, doe come unto them. As for example: The Church of God (forsooth) in the *Black Fryers*, doth consist, besides that parish, of a number of men and Merchaunts wives, dispersed here and there throughout the whole Citie. Bee content to heare the depositions, that are taken to like purpose. *Maister Snape affirmed* (as *Richard Holmes* and *Richard Hawgar* have deposed,) that here one, and there one, picked out of the profane and common multitude, and put apart to serve the Lord, maketh the Church of God, and not the generall multitude. *Maister Johnson* saith, that the brethren of the laitie doe seldome come to their own parish Churches, nor receive the communion there, otherwise then they are compelled for feare of trouble. For they account those their pastors onely, whom they do so chuse. And *Maister Edmonds*, upon his experience in London. The people of this brotherhood, do seldome come to their owne parish Churches, otherwise then for feare to incurre some danger of lawes: neither do they accompt the Minister of their parishes, to be any of their pastors properly: except he be some one of the brethren Ministers, before specified, or very effectually inclining that way.

It is likewise to be observed, that if any of this faction, brotherhood, or sisterhood, do lie dangerously sicke, they do seldome or never send for their owne pastors to visite them: nor move them to pray for them publikely, in their owne parish, as neglecting their prayers: but do send to the Readers abroad, whom they have chosen for their pastors, both to come unto them, and to pray with them, and for them, in their Assemblies.

This also is to bee observed, that the stricter sort of this crue, when they lie at the point of death, will have no bell tolled for them: and many of them do take order before their death: that afterwards, they be not buried in any Church, that there be no Sermon, nor any manner of buriall used, which is prescribed.

CHAP.

Chap. XVI.

A ridiculous pretence of lawes: with a recapitulation of the summe of this third booke.

AS they countenance these their conventicles, and unlawfull assemblies before specified, with the name of *the Church:* so, with the like boldnesse, (to the same purpose) some of them are not ashamed to affirme: that by the doctrine of the Church of *England*, and by the lawes and statutes of this Realm, the present government of the Church of *England*, under her Majesty, by *Archbishops* and *Bishops*, is to be accounted wicked and unlawfull, and withall (in effect) that by the said doctrine, lawes and statutes, all the former proceedings, decrees, &c. of the brethren, are to be maintained and justified. As by the particular proofes following, it will appeare.

The offices a *of Lord Archbishops and Bishops, &c.* (saith Martin Junior) *are condemned, by the doctrine of the Church of England. The doctrine that condemneth the places of Lord Bishops* b *is approved by the statutes of this Realme, and her Majesties prerogative royall. To bee* c *a Lord Bishop is directly against the statute, 13. Elizabeth. According* d *to the doctrine of the Church of England, our Prelates have no authority to make Ministers, or to proceed to any ecclesiasticall censure: their* e *citations, processes, excommunications, &c. are neither to bee obeyed nor regarded. Men ought* f *not to appeare in their Courts: a* g *man being Excommunicated by them ought not to seeke any absolution at their hands.* And in the behalfe of the brethren, he doth also further affirme: *that by the* h *said doctrine of the Church of England &c. All Ministers bee of equall authority*

a Martin Iun.
b Thes. 49.
c Thes. 50.
d Thes. 78.
e Thes. 82.
f Thes. 83.
g Thes. 84.
h Thes. 72.

authority: that the godly Ministers *ought to ordaine those, that would enter into that function, without any leave of the prelates, and not so much as once to suffer them to take any approbation of the prelates: that* every Minister is bound to preach the Gospel, *notwithstanding the inhibition of the Bishops: that a man being once made a Minister, is not to be kept backe from preaching, by the inhibition of any creature: and that by the said doctrine, &c. all* Ministers are bound by subscription, &c. to disavow the Hierarchie of Bishops.

When you shall reade these strange assertions, so farre passing any ordinary bounds of common modestie: thinke with your selves, that it is no marvaile, to see their writings so full of authorities. For I do assure you, that even in the like sort, and with the same sincerity and faithfulnesse, doe they alledge for their platformes, both Scriptures, Councels, Fathers and Histories.

Moreover, what with the pretence of Gods law, of mans law, and I know not of what law, they have been suffered to go so farre against all lawes: that now they have taken such heart, as that some of them are not affraid to affirme (and that in print, because the people might take notice of it:) that there is no Authority, which may lawfully suppress their foresaid proceedings. *No Magistrate (saith one of the brotherhood) may lawfully mayme or deforme the body of Christ, which is the Church: no lawfull Church government is changeable, at the pleasure of the Magistrate: of necessity all christian Magistrates are bound, to receive this government, &c.*

And thus hitherto you have seen the proceedings of our English reformers according to their Ringleaders actions in Scotland: they have had their draughts of Discipline: they have subscribed a particular book for England: they have put their former platformes, and their said particular booke, (for the most part of it,) in practise, as neare as they could: they

Book 3. *English Scottizing, for Discipline by Practise.* 127

they have had their meetings and *Synods*, generally throughout all the land: they have made decrees and conclusions, not onely to further their owne conspiracy, but also to overthrow the present government of the *Church*: they have had in some place their *Elders*: they have exempted themselves from the ecclesiasticall government in this Realme, accounting the same, (in some respects,) to bee *Antichristian* and so not to bee obeyed, and (in some other) to bee a meere civill, and *a Parliament Church-government*: and in that regard, onely after a sort, to bee yeelded unto, for their better and *safer standing*, in their owne seditious and Consistorian wayes. They have by their false glosses, seduced many of her Majesties subjects: they have combined themselves together, into a strange brotherhood: they challenge to their unlawful and seditious Assemblies, the true and most proper name of *the Church*.

They say their doings are according to law.

They affirme (in effect) that no Magistrate may lawfully overthrow that which they have builded, in asmuch, as now it is said, that the [a] *Bishops, in seeking* by the authority which her Majestie hath given and confirmed unto them, to maintaine (as they are bound) the present Church-government and state, established by her highnesse lawes within this Realme, and to suppresse and reforme their schismaticall and seditious disorders, and such like, are the disturbers of the peace of the Church: that the Bishops begin ne *the* [b] *quarrell* in disquieting of them, *who in towne and country, were very greatly at unity, and tooke sweet counsell together, for the profiting of the Church.* That [c] *the Bishops are the schismatikes, and not they: that the crime of schisme, which the prelates would fasten upon them, doth justly cleave to the Bishops: and that* [d] *Bishops may be discharged by the Church.*

And they have entred already into this consideration,

[a] The humble motion pa.84.

[b] The humble motion pa.84.

[c] Epistle to the discovery of R.B. &c.

[d] Register pa.69.

how

128 *English Scottizing, for Discipline by Practise.* Book 3.

how Archbishops, Bishops, Chauncellors, Deanes, Canons, Archdeacons, Commissaries, Registers Apparitors &c. (All which, by their said pretended reformation, must be thrust from their livings) should be provided for, that the common wealth be not thereby pestred with beggars.

Whereby it appeareth, that (in their owne conceits) they have already attained their soveraignty. They and their conventicles (forsooth) are the true Church, and all England besides is in a schisme.

So as now it may bee dayly expected, when these godly brethren, for a full conclusion of their attempts, will take upon them, (as their Masters did in *Scotland*) to discharge the estate of *Bishops*, and to direct their commissioners, to her most excellent Majestie, commanding both her, and her Highnesse most honourable *Privie Councell*, under the paine of excommunication, to appoint no *Bishops* hereafter, because they have concluded that state to bee unlawfull: and that furthermore her *Highnesse* under the same penaltie, shall not presume from henceforth, either any longer to maintaine the present *Antichristian Church-government*, or once to attempt the overthrowing of theirs. And thus much of this matter, viz. concerning our English reformers, and their imitation of the Ministers of *Scotland*, in that seeing they could not prevaile with their suites and supplications to her Majesty and the Parliament, for the setting up of their Discipline: they have taken upon them to doe it themselves.

The end of the third Booke.

THE FOURTH BOOKE OF DISCIPLINARY GROUNDES and Practises.

Chap. I.

Some of them seeme to grow desperate, and propound to themselves a strange example to follow, for the advauncing of their Discipline.

AS the Ministers of *Scotland* with their adherents, finding sundry impediments, and in their foresaid proceedings, and in the setting-up of their Discipline, did grow to bee very angry, and there-upon often-times before they came to armes or violence, did cast out many great speeches and threatnings (as it hath beene before declared:) even so also it fareth now rightly, with our *Disciplinarians* in *England*. They threaten and bragge above measure, what shall come to passe: and I pray God they bee suffered to goe no further.

One of the brethren, (in the name of the rest,) complaining that they are oppugned, and (as hee saith) persecuted, desireth, *that the same may be provided for*: and addeth therewithall

130   *Eng. Scottizing for Discipline by threatnings.*   Book 4.

2 admonit. pa. 59.   withall these words. *It is the case already of many a thousand in this land: yea it is the case of as many as seeke the Lord aright, &c. Great troubles will come of it, if it bee not provided for.*

None seeke the Lord aright but this *brotherhood*. Great joy of them. But what troubles meane they? That, another seemeth to cleare; where hee sayeth, that they can endure no such hard dealing, as is used against them any longer.

Suppl. pa. 61.   *Alas* (saith hee) *wee are never able to stand against the poverty, losses, imprisonment, discountenance, by our superiors, that our brethren have sustained, &c. Never able to swallow up the slanders, and bitter names of Puritans, precisians, traitors, seditious Libellers, &c.* Why? what will you doe?

The best that can bee gathered of his words, is this: *Come* (saith he) *let us make a Captaine, and returne againe into Egypt.* If they have not their minds, the danger may be (which in deed will bring some troubles) that they are not unlike to become either *Atheists* or *Papists*.

Shortly after the strange attempt before mentioned that was made against the King of *Scotland*, Anno 1585. by ten thousand of his own people at *Sterling*, (whereby the Consistorian *Ministers* prevailed, aswell against their Soveraigne, as against their *Bishops*, for the advancing of their *Presbyteries*.) there came out a rayling *Dialogue* here in *England*, published abroad in print, and scattered by the brotherhood throughout the whole Realme.

This *Dialogue* is intituled, *The state of the Church of England laid open in a conference, betweene Diotrephes* (representing the person of a *Bishop*,) *Tertullus a Papist*, (brought in to plead for the orders of our Church,) *Demetrius an Usurer* (signifying such as live by unlawfull trades:) *Pan-*

Book 4. *Engl.Scottizing, for Discipline by threatnings* 131

ry man for his gaine:) and *Paul a Preacher of the word of God*: sustayning the place and persons of the *Consistoriall* brethren.

Where, (by the way,) see againe the account they make of all that doe maintaine the present state of the Church: they are but *ambitious wordlings*, *Papists*, *Livers by unlawfull trades*, and *men pleasers*. But themselves are *Apostles*.

In this *Dialogue*, *Paul* is set forth as a man desirous (upon the *Inne-keepers* motion,) to heare some good newes from *Scotland*: who meeting with the *Bishop*, hee useth him according to the Consistorian humor: that is, most proudly, most spitefully, and most slanderously. Hee condemneth both the calling of *Bishops* as *Antichristian*, and censureth all their proceedings, as wicked, Popish, unlawfull, and cruell. Hee affirmeth that all the good, that hath beene done for the present flourishing estate of the Gospel in *England*, *hath* [a] *beene brought to passe, by those men,* *whom the Bishops despise, and by that course which they were ever enemies unto*. He saith, that [b] *very many of all degrees, are fully perswaded in the matters of reformation, and that he is perswaded, this will come of it, viz. that he shall see the governement of the Church (by the rules of their Discipline) set up before it be long*.

[a] F.1
[b] F.1

The *Bishop* is supposed to have beene sent out of *England* into *Scotland*, for the suppressing of the *Presbyteries* there: and so is made, upon his returne homeward, to bee the reporter of the *Scottish* affaires, and withall to signifie his great feare, lest hee and the rest of the *Bishops* in *England*, should bee served shortly, as the *Bishops* had lately beene in *Scotland*, namely at *Edinburgh* and Saint *Andrewes*, &c.

Ah (saith the pretended *Bishop*) *my host*, the *Puritans*

S 2 *in*

132 *Engl. Scottizing for Discipline, by threatnings.* Book 4

in *Scotland* have got-up their *Discipline*, and utterly overthrown all the soveraignty of *Bishops*: by which they prevailed so mightily, that we feared our fall in *England* shortly to ensue. Whereupon I was sent, together with this my friend (*Tertullus,*) who came out of *France* into *England*, to goe and seeke the subversion of their great *Assemblies*, and the rest of their jurisdiction: wherein I prevailed a while, but now it is worse then ever it was. And it came so to passe, because the whole land cried for *Discipline* againe; and the noble men so stifly did stand to it: and lastly the *Ministers* that came home from *England*, dealt so boldly with the *King*, that I was utterly cast out, without all hope ever to doe any good there againe, and now I make home-ward in haste, least I lose all there also.

Here you have the brethrens approbation of the aforesaid attempt in *Scotland*: whereby it is apparent, that if they shall bee able to bring the people to such a kind of clamor, and the Nobility to such a manner of stifnesse, they can bee well content for their parts, to have her Majesty used, as the *Scottish King* was: for it is according to their *Geneva* Divinity.

Tertullus the *Papist*, hee is made the *Bishops* onely Counsellour, in the whole course of the government of our Church: by whose advice, the author of the *Dialogue* saith, that the *Bishops* doe beare with the Popish recusants, and that so many wayes are sought to suppresse the Puritanes. This *Tertullus*, together with the *Host* and the *Usurer*, doe relate to the *Bishop* those occurrents in *England*, which had fallen out and hapned in his absence. And upon the occasion of this question, asked by the *Bishop*, viz. *Have not the Bishops yet suppressed the Puritans, neither with countenance, nor by authority?* *Tertullus* maketh this answer: *Suppressed? no, my Lord: a friend of mine writ unto me, that one of their preachers said in the pulpit, hee was*

perswaded

Book 4. Engl. Scottizing for Discipline, by threatings. 133
perswaded that there were a 100000. of them in England, and that the number of them increased dayly in every place, of all estates and degrees.

Is it not time for the Magistrates to looke about them? They do take it in scorne to be thought so weake, as that they could be suppressed. Be it they flatter themselves therein, yet their desire is apparent, that (if they bee suffered, and shall ever be able) they will bring it to that passe. And if this be not a necessary consequent of the premisses, my judgement faileth me. But to proceed.

CHAP. II.

Of their Doctrine for making a reformation themselves, and how the people must be thrust into that action.

Bout foure yeares since, it should seeme that some of the brethren, were of opinion, that they had dealt long enough in the practice of their Discipline, after such a secret manner: and that then they were bound in dutie to proceed to the publike exercise of it, notwithstanding any danger, that might thereby ensue. For thus one of them writeth: *Our Zeale to Gods glory, our love to his Church, and the due planting of the same, in this horheaded age should be so warme and stirring in us, as not to care what adventure we give, and what censures we abide, &c. The Iesuits & Seminaries, their diabolicall boldnes will cover our faces with shame, &c.* And after also in the same letter. *We cannot be discharged, of great disloyalty to our comming Christ, except we proceed*

Payne

134 *Eng. Scottizing, for Discipline by threatnings.* Book 4.

ceed with practise, and so to further the Lords cause by suffering: forasmuch as that dutiful suffering, for so honourable a matter, is as sure a signe of subjection, as obeying, the time so urging that bounden duty. It is verily more then time to Register the names of the fittest and hottest brethren round about our severall dwellings, whereby to put Maister Snecanus godly counsell in execution: viz. *Si quis objiciat, &c.* If any man object, that the setting up, and the lawfull practice of the Discipline in the Church is hindred by the civill Magistrate, let the Magistrate bee freely and modestly admonished of his duty. If hee esteeme to be accounted either a godly or a Christian Magistrate, without doubt hee will admit wholesome counsels. But if hee doe not, yet let him bee more exactly instructed, that he may serve God in feare, and bend his authority to the defence of the Church and of Gods glory. Marry, if by this way there happen no good successe, then let the Ministers of the Church execute their office, according to the appointment of Christ: For they must rather obey God then men. In this last point, we have dolefully failed, which now or never standeth us in hand to prosecute with all celerity, without lingring and staying so long for Parliaments.

This advice of *Paines* was thought by the brethren, (as I guesse) to be somewhat too rash: For of likely-hood they could not find at that time so sufficient a number of such *hot brethren,* as might serve their turne. Whereupon (as I suppose) out commeth the decrees of the *Warwick-shire Classes,* that for the increasing of the said number, *every Minister,* (as occasion served,) should teach the Discipline unto the people, as well as the other parts of the Gospel. And for the moderating of *Paines* too hasty advice, it was thus determined: *Nondum solicitandum esse publicè universum cætum ad praxim Disciplinæ, donec melius instituantur homines in ejus cognitione.* that is, As yet the whole multitude are not to be allured (publikely) to the practice of the Discipline, untill men be

better

Book 4. *Eng. Scottizing for Discipline by threatnings.* 135

better instructed in the knowledge of it: As though, for the answering of *Payne*, they had said; that when by that means they had gotten a sufficient number to assist them, then his counsell should be followed.

For you must understand, that their chiefest trust is reposed in the people, as it may be further made more plaine unto you by the deposition of Maister *Edmonds*, whose words I will set downe, as they remaine in record. *I doe well remember* (saith he) *that after I had left that company,* meaning the London *Assemblies, meeting with Maister* Field, *I talked with him, what harme was already done, by inveighing against the present state of the* Church, *and by their proceedings, in beating this their new reformation into the heads of the common people, because they were already growen thereby amongst themselves, into great divisions; very contemptuous, insolent, and intractable, &c Whereunto hee answered, Tush, hold your peace: seing we cannot compass these things by suit nor dispute; it is the multitude and people that must bring them to passe.* But I will leave their endevours a while, how they may seduce the people, and enter into a discourse of their further proceedings.

CHAP. III.

They would have the Nobility and the inferiour Magistrats to set up their discipline & of their supplication with a 100000 *hands.*

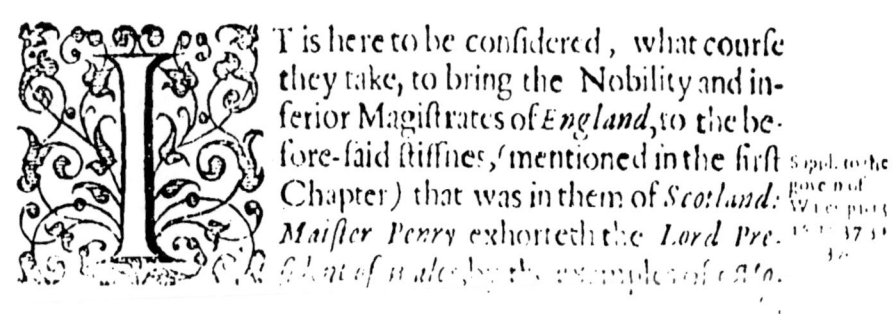

T is here to be considered, what course they take, to bring the Nobility and inferior Magistrates of *England*, to the before-said stiffnes, (mentioned in the first Chapter) that was in them of *Scotland.* Maister *Penry* exhorteth the *Lord President of Wales, by the example of Cato.*

ses, Jehosuah, David, Salomon, Jehosophat, Hezechiah, Josue, Nehemiah, &c. and to take in hand their pretended reformation, in that country: proving that he hath authority thereunto, because hee *is a governour under God*, and that if hee refused so to doe; *hee could have no commission to rule there, in that thereby Christ being rejected, he was become but the Lieutenant of Sathan.* Here you have *Allobrogicall*, and *Consistoriall* stuffe, able of it selfe, (if it were received) to fill all Christian kingdomes, with all kind of mutinies, sedition, and rebellion. They would make the *inferior Magistrates, under their Soveraigne to beleeve*, that they had (for their times, and *within their limits*,) as absolute authoritie, as if they themselves were fully Princes there: and were not many wayes restrayned, by the supreme Magistrate. Surely if they shall bee able, by these and such like perswasions, to draw unto them the *Justices* of *Peace*, the *Sheriffes* or *Lieutenants* of every *Shire*, (and so make them the executioners of their good pleasures and platformes, without any further Commission or warrant from her Majestie:) they shall not need to expect either Prince, or Parliament, but may throw downe, and set up, as great builders doe, whatsoever shall bee most agreeable, to the mutabilitie of their owne affections.

And whereas an objection might have beene made, that if either the Noblemen, Gentlemen, or people should take upon them to cast down the *Bishops*, and to reforme the Church, according to their raigning frenzy, without her Majesties commandement, that in so doing they should greatly disturbe the state of the Realme, and highly offend her most excellent Majestie: these points are both of them passed over with a snuffe, and with great disdaine, as being no such impediments, as ought to hinder the valiant courage

<small>Goodman with the consent of the Generants &c. p. 114. 115.</small>

Book 4. *English Scottizing, for Discipline by threatnings.* 137
rages of *Consistorian* subjects. *I tell you true,* (saith one of *Martin Jun.*
their Captaines) *I thinke it a great blessing of God, that hath* Epilog.
raised up Martin *to hold tackling with the* Bishops, *that you
may have some time of breathing, or rather a time to gather courage and Zeale, &c. to set upon these enemies, &c. For if, as
hitherto you have, you be so loth, for disturbing of our state, forsooth, and the offending of her Majesty, not only to speak against
but even utterly to reject this* Hierarchy of our Bishops, *even to
have no more to do with it, then with the seat of the beast: you
shall declare unto our children, that God can set up, but a company of white-liuered souldiers, &c.* Forsooth if this exhortation be according to their Discipline, it ought no longer
to bee termed Christs, (as they terme it) but the Divels
Discipline. And yet, because they would not have her *Martin sen.*
Majesty altogether neglected, another of their *Lieutenants* can bee content, that (before their souldiers mentioned should beginne the skirmish) there might bee
first, (as it were) for a parlee, some little overture
of duty signified: that, if (as yet) her Highnesse
would bee ruled by them, they would desist. To
this purpose hee moveth all the *Puritanes,* (as hee termeth them) in *England* both Lords, Knights, Gentlemen, Ministers and people, to offer a supplication to
her Majesty; in effect, for the full obtayning of all their
desires.

To this (saith he) *an hundred thousand hands would be gotten, &c. and then thou* (speaking to his Reader) *may well think,
what a stroke so many would strike together, &c. It should appeare, that they are not few, and of small reputation, but in a
manner the strength of our land, and the sinew of her Majesties
royall government, which our Bishops do falsly note with the
names of Puritanes, The consideration whereof, I tell thee, even
in policie, would make that this their sutt should not bee hastily*
T *rejected,*

rejected, especially in such a time, as wherein we now live, in danger of our enemies abroad, and therefore had need of no causes of discouragement at home. I like it well when men will deale plainly: You see indeed their hearts. And is it not then evident whereat they aime? *In such a time no policie?* Indeed the returne of the *Spaniard* was then expected. No need then of discouragement at home? Why? wanting your desires, would you have taken no part, if the *Spaniard* had come? or purposed you to have made a more ready passage for him, by rebelling at home, before he should have come? or would you have joyned with him, if hee had come? or meant you thereby, (through terror) to have enforced her Majesty to your purposes, lest you should have taken some of these courses? Chuse which of them you list, 'the best is seditious.

Chap. IIII.

Presuming upon some unlawfull assistance, they use very violent words.

How true it is, that they have a hundred thousand ready at their direction, I know not: but they have surely too many: if the companion of the brotherhood, that sent his humble motion abroad, may bee herein beleeved: *Thousands (he saith) do sigh for this Discipline, and ten thousand have sought it; and approved and worthy men of every shire, have consented unto it.*

But certaine it is, such is their hope to thrust the people, with the rest of their confederates, into some unlawfull execution of their distempered designements, that they
are

Book 4. *English Scottizing, for Discipline by threatnings.* 139.

are come to a wonderfull resolution and assurance, as having almost (in their owne conceipts,) obteined, already, the very Scepter of their Kingdome. *The Eldership is at hand,* (saith the *humble motioner.*) And againe, using reasons why the state here in *England* should presently embrace their government, hee falleth upon these two points, (jumping justly with the *Scottish* Ministers Logique mentioned before by *Diotrephes*, the pretended *Bishop*,) viz. *the people are inflamed with Zeale:* and (as it seemeth) the second reason dependeth upon the first, that is, *because it is hard, dangerous, and impossible to stand against it.* In effect, the people crie for the *Discipline*, and therefore it must needs prevaile. Indeed they have slaunderously set out supplications and complaints in the name of the commonaltie; thereby to terrifie their withstanders. But I trust the people generally are not so mad, although there bee some that are strangely bewitched. Unto this conceipt of the peoples readinesse it seemeth to mee, that *M. Snape* had relation, when hee used these words following, as they are set downe by the oathes of some of them, to whom he spake them. *How say you* (quoth hee) *if wee,* meaning himselfe and his fellow Ministers, with their adherents, *devise a way, whereby to shake off all the Antichristian yoke, and government of the Bishops: and will joyntly together erect the discipline and government all in one day: but peradventure it will not be yet, this yeere and a halfe.* Another, (of his more then superabundant charity) foreseeing the mischiefes that are ready to fall, by his brethrens procurement, upon the Bishops of this Realme, giveth them warning to be gone in time. *Be packing Bishops,* (saith he) *you strive in vaine: you are laid open already.*

Fryers and Monkes were not so bad. Look to your selves; for my sonnes will not see their father thus persecuted at your

Holmes, Hawgar, &c.

Epistle to Mart epitome.

T 2 *hands.*

140 English Scottizing, for Discipline by threatnings. Book 4.

W.P. hands. *Wee protest* (say the authors of a certaine supplication, drawen to her Majesty, and found in one of the brethrens studies: but hee will not confesse, by whose advice it was penned:) *We protest (say they) vnto your Majesty, that we will bee no longer subject vnto the Bishops vnlawfull and*

Epist. to the Demonst. *vsurped authority, &c. wherefore let them not looke for it at our hands.* And another. *The truth will prevaile* (speaking of the Discipline) *in spight of your teeth* (meaning the Bishops,) *and all other adversaries of it.* Likewise another dealeth as charitably with the Common-wealth, as his fellow

Martin iun. Thes.98, to 9 100, 105. did with the *Bishops*: that is, hee warneth to take heed: saying, *that it will be very dangerous to our state, to maintaine two contrary factions: that the Magistrates are then bound, even for the quieting of our state, to put downe the one, that those, that stand for the Discipline, neither can nor will giue it ouer, (so as they will not bee put downe) and that the said Magistrates cannot maintaine the corruption of our Church, namely Archbishops and Bishops, without the discontentment of their subjects.*

And another: *wee have sought to advance this cause of God, by humble suit to the Parliament, by supplication to your Convocation house, by writing in defence of it, and by challenging to dispute for it: seeing none of these meanes used by us have prevailed, if it come in by that meanes which will make all your hearts to ake, blame your selves.*

Martins protestation. And to conclude. *In this one point* (saith another) *the Bishops are of my minde: viz. that reformation cannot well come to our Church, without bloud.* Let the place be throughly considered. The words are ambiguously set downe of purpose to cover (in some sort) the cruelty, which lurketh in their owne hearts. For in my simple judgement, his speeches can have no other good and coherent sense, then this, viz. that as the Bishops do thinke (as hee slanderously deemeth)

meth) that there can bee no reformation of the *Puritanes* disordered proceedings, without the bloud of some of their brotherhood: so hee is of minde, that the reformation which hee and his companions do seeke for, cannot be attained unto, without the bloud of some of those, that do withstand their platformes. It is true that hee there onely prosecuteth the cruell opinion, which he ascribeth to the *Bishops*: saying that *no bloud can handsomely be spilt, unlesse they be the butchers*. But he passeth cunningly by his owne minde, as very well knowing his companions capacities. Indeed, if they do take upon them to spill bloud, they cannot (thanks bee to God) as yet, do it handsomely. The Lord of his infinite mercie grant that their opportunities, to such a mischiefe, do never serve them better, then hitherto they have done.

Chap V.
Upon Cartwrights committing to prison, some strange attempts were looked.

Besides prayers to prevent such outrages (as are mentioned in former chapters) there must bee other meanes diligently looked into. For out of question, it is high time. Every one is acquainted with the execution of *Hacket*, but few do understand the secrets of those attempts. They stretch much further then they are supposed.

You may remember, the *Disciplinarie* mens Doctrine (before mentioned) viz. that when Princes grow to be tyrants, (whereof seditious spirits will bee the Judges,) and that the inferiour Magistrates will not do their duties, the people then, (if any *Jonathan* will step forth, to bee their Captaine) are bound to joyne themselves unto him, and

Buch. de jure regn. 57.
Goodman. pag. 185.
Junius Brutus. 170.
Beza de authori. magist. intubd p 97.

142 *English Scottizing, for Discipline by threatnings.* Book 4.

I.P. Of obedience. Whitting. hams preface Goodman. pag. 196. I.P. 116.

may use the sword in their owne right : or otherwise some private man, that is moved with zeale *extra ordinem*, may execute vengeance, upon Prince or Potentate, Idolater, wicked persons, &c. even as the spirit shall move him. The which doctrine (as I said) they take upon them to confirme, out of the Scriptures, by these examples, viz. of *Phineas*, who in zeale killed the Adulterers: of *Ahud*, who in zeale killed King *Eglon* in his private chamber: of *Iael*, who in zeale killed *Sisera*: of *Matathias*, who in zeale killed a *Jew* for committing Idolatry: and of the same *Matathias*, who in the same zeale killed likewise, at the same time, the Kings Commissioners, that commanded the people to conforme themselves to the Kings proceedings, &c.

To those that know these principles, how can it bee either obscure or difficult, what they are both to thinke and judge, when they shall heare of any *extraordinary* callings, and secret motions in private men? whereby they shall take upon them, (through the assistance of giddy and seduced male-contents) to correct and amend, to set up and throw downe, to deliver and restraine, to punish and execute, how, what, where, when and whom, &c. according to their owne pleasures: and all under pretence of such directions, as they shall affirme that the holy Ghost doth minister unto them.

Upon the proceedings, held by course of law against *Udall* and some others : and likewise by reason that certaine Preachers, but especially Master *Cartwright*, being called before her Majesties Commissioners in causes Ecclesiasticall, for their aforesaid undutifull proceedings, were (upon just occasions) committed to prison; the matter was greatly grudged at, and so taken to heart, amongst the reforming and zealous brotherhood, as that many devises and complots, were (as it seemeth) in deliberation not

onely

Book 4. *English Scottizing, for Discipline by force.* 143.
onely how the said prisoners might (for the present) bee defended and delivered, but also how thereupon they might proceed for the setting up of their Discipline. To this purpose, in mine opinion these words of *Wiggintons* are very pertinent. *Master Cartwright is in the Fleete for refusall of the oath (as I heare) and Master Knewstubs is sent for, and sundry worthy Ministers are disquieted, who have beene spared long. So that we look for some bickering ere long, and then a battell; which cannot long endure.* How farre these words may bee drawne, I leave it to be considered of, by those that can discerne of such like kind of phrases. This I can assure you of, that (upon what grounds I know not) through the course which was held by the Magistrates here against the said prisoners, there was great expectation, and as it were a hope conceived by their favourers in another countrey, of some bickering amongst us, (about that time,) as *Wigginton* writeth of. Thus a man that hath beene of especiall account in *Scotland*, did write unto a friend of his in *England*: *I attend your next answer, aswell of the estate of your Church, as of all other affaires. For there is here great word of sundry uproares, which I trust be false, or repressed in due season by her Majesty.*

Wigginton, to Porter at Lancaster, 6. Novemb. 1590.

P.A.7. Decemb. 1590.

But that passeth all (to this purpose,) which falleth out most apparently, by the view taken of such letters and papers as were found upon the apprehension of *Hacket* and his Prophets.

Chap. VI.

One Edmond Coppinger took upon him to work Cartwrights, &c. deliverance: he pretendeth an extraordinary calling and acquainteth divers with it: one Gibson a Scot. P. Wentworth, Cartwright, Wigginton, Charke, Travers, Egerton, &c.

Whilest

144 *English Scottizing, for Discipline by threatnings.* Book 4.

Whilest some were devising of one way, and some of another, for the good of the said prisoners, &c. One *Edmond Coppinger*, with his familiars, could finde no meanes to bee looked for, except it might please God, according to the foresaid positions, to stirre up some zealous brethren, by some extraordinary calling, to effect their desires. This cogitation (as it seemeth) no sooner grew upon them, but that by and by they felt, (as they thought) in themselves some certaine slender instigations to such a heauenly purpose. It appeareth that towards the latter end of *December*, 1590. *Coppinger*, *Arthington*, and *John Bentley*, [a] a Master *Knightlies* man, did hold a fast at one *Thomas Lancasters* house, a schoolemaster in *Shoe-lane*. It began upon the *Saturday* at night, and held till *Sunday* at night. In the time of this fast, viz. the *Saturday* [b] at night, *Coppinger* (as he said) found himselfe *very extraordinarily exercised, &c. with a wonderfull zeale, to set forth Gods glory any wayes which lawfully he might enter into.* At that time also, (I mean at that last fast) *Arthington had likewise his extraordinary calling.* Thus *Coppinger* did write of his matter to *Lancaster*: the letter was also subscribed unto by *Arthington*. In [c] *your house, in your presence, and partly by your meanes; I had my first extraordinarie calling, and of the same minde is my brother Arthington.* *Coppinger* the next day after the said fast, did ride into *Kent*, and upon his returne (which was with some speed) hee signified unto his fellow-fasters, how he had beene extraordinarily called, both before his going, the said *Saturday at night*; and also in his journey, since he departed from them : viz: how God had *revealed* [d] unto him such a secret mystery, as was wonderfull. *By the way* (saith hee) *as I rid, I fansied to my selfe, that there was leave given mee to speake to*

God

[a] Copping. examined, 19 of July. Arthing. discourse.
[b] Copping. to T.C.
[c] Copping. and Arthing. to Lancaster, the 15. of July. 1591.
[d] Arthing. discourse.
Cop. to T.C.

Book 4.   *English Scottizing, for Discipline by force.*   145

God, in a more familiar manner then at any time before: also I perswaded my selfe, that his spirit did give me many strange directions, wherein the Lord would use me to do service to his most glorious Majesty, and to his Church. Concerning the substance of his said revelation, he also told *Arthington* and *Lancaster* thus much: viz. that he knew a way how to bring the Queene to repentance, and to cause all her Councell and Nobles to do the like out of hand, or else detect them to bee traytors that refused. Arthingtons discourse.

After the relation of these things, within a day or two, this *Coppinger* and *Arthington* held another fast by themselves. Whereupon (saith *Coppinger*) *I was againe stirred up to such businesse of such importance, as in the eyes of flesh and bloud, was likely to bring much danger to my selfe, and unlikely to bring any good successe to the Church of God.* Cop. to T.C.

Of these his instigations, or revelations, hee writ to some preachers in the Realme: and to some without: as namely a letter the last day of December, 1590. to one *Gibson*, a kinde of preacher in *Scotland*: Wherein hee greatly complaineth of the present state of our Church, and desireth of him to bee instructed from the brethren there, in divers points, concerning an extraordinary calling. *The state of our Church* (saith hee) *groweth worse and worse: our zealous Ministerie and Magistracie are daily disgraced and displaced: the meanes of help is taken away, except that God would either move her Majesty inwardly, shee being bereaved of those holy helps which Gods servants enjoy in the publike exercise of religion: or else stirre up some faithfull Zorobabel or Nehemiah, to let her see how the Lords house lyeth waste, and how usurpers of Antichristian tyranny do keepe Christ Jesus from governing in his Kingdome.* And then hee addeth: *My selfe am acquainted with some, who, to do service herein, would adventure the losse of their lives, so that* Cop. to T.C. Copping. to Gibson.

V   they

they might have warrant from the word, for their so doing, and have approbation by the Church. And to this end they fancie to themselves to have received an extraordinary calling, wherein they feare to be abused by Sathan. Then followeth his petition. And therefore I, though most unworthy, have adventured to write unto you, to beseech you in the bowels of Christ Jesus, to have conference with such as are most able to advise you on our behalfe, and to returne answer, how a man may examine himselfe in this matter, and what bee the extraordinary things which must be in him that is so called: what course he is to take, to have his extraordinary calling knowne, first to himselfe, and then to the Church.

After hee had sent away this Letter into *Scotland*, hee began to draw his doubts into some method, and did propound them all in eight questions. The chiefe summe whereof, is this, *Whether in these dayes, and in this countrey, where there is but preaching here and there, where the Discipline is not established, but oppugned by the publike Magistrates, whether there bee place for any extraordinary calling immediately from God, of workers and helpers to his Church, &c.* These questions thus contrived hee sent them to his old acquaintance *Wigginton*: who justly, according to *Coppingers* humour, answered them all affirmatively; as his answers are to bee shewed under his owne hand, and as *Coppinger* did also write unto Master *Cartwright*; the effect of which Letter will follow in course.

Upon *Coppingers* receipt of this answer, that there was high time for such extraordinary callings, *presently after*

Cop.to T.C. *there was another fast procured by Coppinger*, for a better conformation of such his manner of calling, and to see if any moe might be drawne thereby into the same conceipt. *This fast was held upon the Wednesday, in a Merchants house*

where

Book 4. *English Scottizing, for Discipline by force.* 147

where Wigginton then lay, and Wigginton himselfe, with three _{Cop. exam.}
or foure others, was present at it. But before this fast was held, ^{19. July.}
meanes was used (saith Coppinger) *to have some notice given to*
some of the Preachers in prison, of the day of their humiliation,
and of their desire to have them commend unto God in their
prayers the holy purposes, which any fearing God, should in time _{Cop. to T.C.}
attempt to take in hand, by seeking the glory of God, and the
good of the Church.

The effect of their prayers in this fast, was this, viz. *They* _{Cop. exam.}
humbly beseech Almighty God, that if he had appointed to use ^{19. July.}
any of them, to do any speciall service to him and his; and that
to that end would extraordinarily call them, that he would seale _{Cop. to T.C.}
up his or their so calling by some speciall manner, and by his ho-
ly spirit, and give such extraordinary graces and gifts, as were
fit for so weighty an action.

How the rest of this company sped hereby, I finde it
not: but *Coppinger* (as hee saith) *was called againe the same* _{Cop. exam.}
night in a dreame. The manner whereof hee thus descri-
beth. *About the middle part of the night, I thought my selfe* _{Cop. to T.C.}
in my sleep, to be carried into Heaven, and there being wonder-
fully astonished with the Majesty of God, and brightnesse of his
glory, I made a loud and most strong noise, &c. since which time
I finde every day more and more comfort, and suppose there is
somewhat in me, &c. to work (he meaneth some strange reformation.)

As before it hath beene partly touched, *Coppinger* did not
onely crave the advice of some Ministers in these his great
actions, (as oft hee termeth them:) but also of such of the
Laity, as hee thought were most fit to joyne with him, or
to advise him: and I doubt not, but that he dealt as plainely with them, as hee had done before with *Davison* a *Scot*,
and others. This doth appeare, in some sort, by a Letter
written unto *Coppinger* by *Peter Wentworth*, the five and
V 2 twen-

twentieth of January 1590. in answer of one sent unto him before, from *Coppinger*. It seemeth that *Coppinger* having desired Master *Wentworth* to come unto him to *London*, that they might conferre together, &c. for answer hee excuseth himselfe in respect of his lamenesse, &c. and *of his debility and weaknesse, to give advice in matters of importance, wherein I perceive* (saith hee) *you are labouring. And further* (saith hee,) *I do assure my selfe, that the purpose tendeth unto the true service of God, and of her Majesty. I beseech you resort to the Lord, to direct your labours both in matter and manner. For an ill manner may marre a good matter. You are in a plentifull soile, where you may use the advice of many godly wise. Use the benefit thereof, and then, as* Josua *said, be bold, and of good courage: feare not to be discouraged.*

Besides it appeareth by a Letter of *Coppingers* to *Thomas Lancaster*, the Schoolemaster, dated the nine and twentieth of *January*: that hee had disclosed (as it should seeme) all the premisses unto diverse of the Ministers of *London*, desiring to have had *some conference with them*: and offering himselfe to be *directed either to proceed, or draw back, as the Church should advise*. But they supposing the *matter to be too hard to be effected*; and *him an unfit man to manage it*, refused to admit of any such conference. In the same Letter, it is also evident, that *Coppinger* had made, *the night before, a rude discourse* (as he termeth it) to *Lancaster* of these matters; which *Lancaster* disliked. And touching some speeches had with Master *Egerton*, thus he there writeth: *Most true it is, that he refused to take triall me, and of my gifts: alledging, that he was a meane ordinary man, &c. and one that could not judge of extraordinary gifts: and withall, most Christianly, wisely, and lovingly perswaded me to be carefull and circumspect over my selfe, to take heed lest I was deceived by the*

subtilty

subtilty of Sathan, and so misse-led; whereby I might endanger my selfe, both for my liberty, estate, and credit, and also be an hinderance to the great cause, which I would seeme to be most desirous to further. But withall he concluded, that he would bee loath the quench the spirit of God in mee, or to hinder my zeale.

In another Letter also, to the said *Lancaster* from *Coppinger*, concerning other his proceedings with *Egerton*, he saith: *it cannot be denied, but that the cause is good, which I desire to be an actor in: but it is said by some, that it is impossible that I should be fit to meddle therein.* Hee also desireth *Lancaster* to deale with *Egerton*, that hee might have *a sight of all the Letters which he (the said Coppinger) had written unto him about these matters.*

About this time it also appeareth, that *Coppinger* fell into some dealings with M. *Cartwright*, concerning the premisses: and that he had sent unto him the questions before mentioned, for to know his resolution, whether it would bee agreeable to *Wiggintons*. Hee writ a Letter unto him, dated the fourth of February 1590. beginning thus:

Right reverend Sir, your most wise and christian counsell, together with offer to take knowledge by writing from me, of such matters as might induce me to suppose my selfe to have received some hope of speciall favour from God, to some speciall use: doth move me more and more to admire his mercies towards me, &c.
In this Letter hee signifieth to M. *Cartwright* (as before I have noted,) the number of their fasts, his severall callings, his writing to some preachers within the Realme, and to some without: and his confirmation by *Wiggintons* said answers, and maketh these petitions unto him: viz. *that the Church (I meane, saith he, your selfe and such as you shall name unto me:) would look narrowly into him, for the triall of his extraordinary calling. If* (saith he) *I be thought to be any wayes*

150 *English Scottizing, for Discipline by force.* Book 4.

mis-led, I crave sharp censuring: If I be guided by Gods spirit to any good end,(as hereafter shalbe adjudged,) I shalbe ready to acquaint you and them with generalities and particularities, so far-forth as you and they be desirous to look into them. And his second petition was, viz. *to have(saith he)your further answer to some questions, wherein I desire to be resolved with your direction also, what hereafter I am to signifie to your selfe concerning the matter it selfe.*

After M. *Cartwright* had received this Letter from *Coppinger*, hee sent unto him a message, *that hee should attempt nothing but by advice, and that hee should bee wise and circumspect.* Besides, it seemeth, that upon *Coppingers* so earnest sute, made as hath beene specified, there was a time appointed that he might be conferred withall. These things do appear to be true by a second letter of *Coppingers* to *Cartwright* the 13. of February: Wherein he greatly complained that *he had beene put back from that service of God and his Church which he had in hand (and that by his friends:)* he desired M. *Cartwright that the day appointed for conference might hold,* and hee addeth this reason: *The danger which some stand in, for their lives, is not unknowne; and if I had not beene letted, I durst have ventured my life, to have procured their release ere now.*

And againe to the same effect, *As I may, I command you in the name of God, that you advise the preachers to deale speedily and circumspectly, lest some bloud of the Saints be shed.* In the end he signifieth, that the next day, he with some others, *did meane to humble themselves in fasting, and that the prisoners did know of it.*

Whilest *Coppinger* was in expectation of the said conference: how it fell out I know not, but (as it seemeth) councell was taken, and the matter over-ruled, that the Ministers appointed should utterly refuse to have any conference
with

[margin: Copping. to T.C. 13. of Febr. 1590.]

Book 4.   English Scottizing, for Discipline by force.   151

with him. Whereupon M. *Cartwright, Travers, Charke,* and *Egerton,* sent him word by M. *Hockenhull, that they would leave him to himselfe, or rather to Sathan: and that they thought him unworthy to bee conferred withall.* And this appeareth by *Coppingers* Letter to *Charke, Travers* and *Egerton,* beginning thus: *Right reverend fathers, &c.* About the delivery of this message, *Coppinger* did after (in some sort) challenge M. *Hockenhull,* and told him also *that seeing hee had beene refused to be conferred withall by those godly, wise, and zealous preachers, who had promised to have had conference with him, &c. occasion thereby was offered unto him to approve himselfe.*

<small>Copping. to Charke, Travers and Egerton.</small>

<small>Cop. to Hockenh. 24. Febr. 1590.</small>

About this time, or a little before, *Coppinger* received a Letter, in answer of his, from *Gibson* (the Scottish Minister above mentioned:) dated from *Pententland in Scotland* the sixth of February 1590. concerning the points of *Coppingers* said Letter unto him: Wherein hee writeth very cunningly, touching *Coppingers* question, and shifteth it over (like his craftf-master) with an indirect and uncertaine answere. But in these points hee is very plaine: viz. that hee *had shewed Coppingers Letter to sundry, that hee had conferred of it with the best of their Ministery: that their Church was not forgetfull to do all good offices, for the weale of the brethren here: that there was a writing ready to send to* Germany *to* Junius, *that hee would travell with some of the good and well affected professors there: that (of his knowledge) travell was to be made with some others, as namely the King of* France, *and that their Ministery would themselves travell with her Majesty.* No doubt if *Junius* or any other, at their request shall take upon them to deale with her highnesse, for men of *Coppingers* humour or for any of those whom he would have delivered, the suggestions (which either are, or must bee made unto them,) are

are like to containe many slanders and untruths. But to go forward.

Chap. VII.

How Coppinger and Arthington came acquainted with Hacket: Of their conference with Jo. Throg. Coppingers letter to Jo. Throg. and his answer.

<small>Hacket to Wigginton, March 15, 0.</small>

Shortly after this time, viz. the 3. of March 1590. *William Hacket,* an old companion of *Wiggintons* did write unto him, and doth comfort him then in prison, with the examples of *Gideons empty pitchers,* of the deliverance *by Moses through the read sea,* and of *Haman that was hanged upon the same gibbet he had prepared for another.* He useth also these words: Master *Wigginton, I desire to communicate my spirit at large with you: but I know not your keeper, &c. Good* M. Wigginton, *make my sound heart knowne to* M. Cartwright, M. Snape, M. Udall M. Lord.

<small>Hackets discourse.</small>

In the *Easter* terme this *Hacket* came up to London, of likelihood to communicate his spirit with *Wigginton,* and to grow into acquaintance with the parties named: but his pretence was, *partly to see what would become of Job Throgmorton, and partly to reckon with Wigginton, about the making of malt betweene them together.* Hee had not beene long *in London,* but hee came to *Wigginton,* who (amongst other discourses) told *Hacket* that there was a *Gentleman* (meaning M. *Coppinger*) *in the City, a very good man, &c.* He describeth him unto *Hacket,* and the matter also hee was entring into: signifying further, how *Coppinger had beene wonderfully discouraged* (in his purposes) *by the Preachers in London*

Book 4. *English Scottizing, for Discipline by force.* 153

London: but that hee (for his part) had not so done. &c. Hee also commended *Arthington* to *Hacket*, to bee an honest man. Then Wigginton *sent for* Coppinger, *and by Gods providence he came forth-with unto him, and* M. Wigginton *willed* Coppinger *and* Hacket *to take acquaintance one of the other, assuring* Coppinger *that he knew* Hacket *to be a man truly fearing God, and such a person, as God might Minister some comfort to* Coppinger *by his conference: that* Hacket *had bin tormented, and that for the credit of* Hackets *sufferings, a hundreth could witness.* About this time also, Arthington *by* Wiggintons *and* Coppingers *meanes* (as he saith) *fell into acquaintance with* Hacket, *meeting first with him at* Mistris Lawsons *house*, M. Job Throgmorton *also being then at* London, *grew into some conference* (as it should seeme) *with these three companions,* Coppinger, Arthington, *and* Hacket: And this is gathered by *Coppingers* letter to *Job Throgmorton*, after his departure from *London* that terme: and by the answer, returned from him under his owne hand, and sealed with his seale of armes. Both the letters are fit to bee considered. Thus *Coppinger* writ unto him, as it appeareth under his owne hand.

My owne deare brother, my selfe and my two brethren, who lately were together with you in Knight-rider *street, do much desire conference with you, which will aske some time. The busines is the Lords own, and he doth deale in it himselfe, in a strange and extraordinary manner, in poore and simple creatures. Much is done since you see us, which you will rejoyce to heare of when we shall meet: and therefore I beseech you as soone as you receive this letter, hasten an answer in writing to my sister* Randolphes *house, at* St. Peters *hill foote, by* Pauls *wharfe. Therein advertise (I beseech you) when I may come to speake with you: for delayes are dangerous, and some of the great enemies begin to be so pursued*

Arthing. ex 19. July 1591.

Arthing. ex 30. of July 1591.

Arthing ex 19. of July 1591.

Where Hacket then lay by Coppingers appointment.

X

sued by God, as they are at their wits end. The Lord make us thankfull for it, who keepe us ever to himselfe, to doe his will and not ours.

Your very loving brother in the
L. most assured to command.

This copie remaineth thus endorsed: *The copie of a letter to M. Job Throgmorton, from E. C.* And now followeth *Throgmortons* letter, being an answer (as I take it) unto Coppingers.

My good brother, &c. (I rejoyce that you will vouchsafe so to account of mee.) Your godly conference at any time, when opportunity shall serve, I will not refuse. And albeit our businesse may hinder us now to meet, yet there is no time overpast, but that it may be performed, when it please God. The next terme (you heare) I must appeare here againe upon my band: at which time you shall find that I wil be glad of your christian conference, or of any other brothers, by whom I may bee enlightened. Lord deliver mee from that pride of heart, to reject or refuse that while I live. That course you speake of, intended by you, I was never (you know) in particular acquainted with. And therefore, for mee to like or dislike a matter, that I had no knowledge of, had beene (I take it) without ground or warrant. Onely I confesse, I heard some buzzes abroad of a sole and singular course, that either you, or some other had plotted in his head, which was greatly feared, and condemned of the brethren. What that was I know not, so had I small reason to speake of it with prejudice. Onely I would wish you, and all that beare good will to the holy cause, in this perilous age of ours, to take both your eyes in your hands, (as they say) and to be sure of your ground and warrant, before you strive to put in execution: For as I like not of coldnesse of zeale, under colour of discretion: so on the other side, I think that this sentence of our Saviour (be ye wise as serpents) was not written in vaine neither, and had great neede to be practised of some in this age. A sanctified cause, (you know) would alwayes have a sanctified course. Our rule and square must be the word of truth, which, so long as we lay before us as our level, we shal not lightly swarve much from the marke. The Lord therefore direct us, in these fearefull and miserable dayes, and let not our infirmities be a bar to his mercies. I know (my good Brother) that the greatest workes of the Lord are wrought by the weakest instruments, lest men should boast in the arme of flesh. And therefore (were it not for my sinnes and unworthinesse) I could easily perswade my selfe, in regard of my weaknesse, that the Lord might effect something by me, who am privy to mine owne wants, and farre short of those good giftes it pleaseth you (of your love) to loade mee with. But this worke, that you speake of (howsoever the instrument bee compassed with weaknesse) must sure be wrought by a more sanctified heart, then my selfe can yet without hypocrisie boast of. And therefore, though in affection and good will I joyne, yet I resigne the honour of the work, to those, that the Lord hath more enabled. The man you speake of (if he be at Oundel) dwelleth hard by a Sister of mine, and thereupon I shall have the better occasion to see him when it please God. Forget me not in your holy Prayers and meditations, and salute good Giles with many thankes, whose debtor I am in the Lord. Blessing upon Sion, confusion upon Babel, haste this 18. of the 5. Moneth.

Ever yours in the Lord.

156 *English Scottizing, for Discipline by force.* Book 4.

Chap. VIII.

Coppinger to Hacket of an appearance in the Star-chamber: his letter to Udall: why Cartwright, &c. refused to confer with him. Cartwright resolved some questions of Coppingers. Of eight preachers that did fast and pray for Coppingers successe.

After some few dayes, that *Hacket* had tarried in *London*, the said Easter terme, he returned home againe to *Oundle*, having first promised *Coppinger*, that hee would come up againe unto him, whensoever hee sent for him. Now *Coppinger*, by his said conferences and acquaintance with *Hacket*, was grown (as he said) *very bold and couragious.* But yet shortly after, viz. (as I thinke) the seventeenth of *May*, hee liked so well of *Hackets* company, that he sent for him againe, to come up unto him: saying, *If Gods spirit direct you to come, come: if not, stay. But write with all speed, and convey your letter, and inclose it in a letter to him, who brought you and me acquainted:* (that was *Wigginton:*) *put not to your name for discovery, &c.* And in the same letter hee sendeth *Hacket* this newes. *The zealous Preachers (as it is thought) are to be in the Star-chamber to morrow.* (I thinke he meaneth the last day of Easter Terme last.) *The L. by his holy spirit be with them, and stay al evil that is intended against them. My selfe, If I can get in, am moved to be there: and I feare, if sentence with severity shall be given, I shall be forced in the name of the great and fearefull God of heaven and earth, to protest against it.* About this time also hee writ a very couragious letter to *Udall* in prison: (for he confesseth it was

written

Book 4.   *English Scottizing, for Discipline by force.*   157

written about ten weekes before his examination, which was the nineteenth of *July*:) In this letter he telleth him, that (*notwithstanding some brethrens hard opinions of him, and other discouragements, yet) now the Lord hath not onely enabled him to fight, but at the length (in some sort) to vanquish and overcome.* Hee signifieth also unto him, that *the next day, there were some few, that purposed to joyne together in a holy fast, in regard of the afflicted Saints in generall, &c.* Hee greatly *commendeth the Ministers cause and sufferings, that are in prison, assuring himselfe that God will blesse all the actions in it.* He saith, *there were diverse out of prison, lying hid, that in this great work were hammering their heads, bestowing their braines, and spending their spirits: who doe hope (in short time) to bee brought forth into the sight of their and your enemies, to defend the cause you stand for: whose presence (God assisting them,) will daunt the enemies more then yours: for that they be men void of learning wisdome and gifts, such as can challenge nothing to themselves, but must give all to God: who in all the greatest workes, that ever have beene wrought, hath used the weakest meanes, lest men should boast in the arme of flesh. And therefore (I beseech you) cheere up your selves in the Lord, for the day of our redemption is at hand: and pray, that the hand of the Lord may be strengthned in them, whom he hath appointed to take part with you in this cause.*

Here (you see) he was growne to a wonderfull resolution: But yet there is another letter of his, that will make the same more evident, and likewise lay open more plainly some of the premisses, then hitherto they have beene. Hee sheweth therein, that hee could be still well contented, *to have some conference with Maister Charke, Maister Travers, Maister Egerton, Maister Gardiner, Maister Phillips, and Maister Couper. But* (saith he) *I make not this suite, for that I would seeke to have approbation from them, or any other living*

Capping to Udall. May 1591.

Hacker and his fellowes

The Copy of Cop letter to a friend 11. May 1591

X 3   *creature,*

creature, but from God himselfe.

You have heard before, how these Ministers have refused to conferre with *Coppinger*. And what should a man thinke the cause might bee? Surely a feare they had, lest he should (by entring into some particulars) bring them within the compasse of his dangerous complots. This may bee necessarily there also gathered, in that as shewing hee could bee content to conferre with the said parties, not because (hee protesteth) that he would seeke any approbation from them: so doth hee likewise remove that doubt, saying, that *he purposed not to acquaint them with the courses, which he purposed by Gods assistance to take in hand, whereby great danger might grow to them, and little good to him: but that they might be witnesses of his humility, &c.*

You have heard also, of one of *Coppingers* petitions to Master *Cartwright*, for his answer to those questions mentioned, that hee had before propounded to *Wigginton*. Whereunto it should seeme, that although at the first hee misliked that motion, yet in the end hee yeelded. *My humble desire to you is* (saith *Coppinger*) *that you (in my name) give great thankes to good Maister Cartwright, for satisfying me in some questions, which at the first, he thought little use to be made of.* Likewise it also appeareth, that Master *Hockenhull* did his aforesaid message unto *Coppinger*, from the preachers, in harder manner then hee had Commission. *For* (saith hee) *his counsell* (that is *Cartwrights*) *and carriage of himselfe the Lord did direct and blesse it unto mee, though the Messenger, &c. in his carriage of himselfe, failed somewhat, both in that he delivered from him, and the rest of the Brethren.* And whereas furthermore in like sort, notice being given to the Ministers in prison of one of *Coppingers* Fasts, it appeared not what regard they had thereof; that point also is now cleared in the same Letter. *I beseech you also give thankes, on my behalfe,*

Book 4. *English Scottizing, for Discipline by force.* 159

behalfe, to the other eight preachers: for upon notice given unto them by some of Gods children, that somewhat was intended to be done, wherein Gods glory might appeare, and request made that the Religious desires, and godly purposes of the faithfull, might be strengthned by their holy prayers: they thereupon, (as it is credibly signified unto me) humbled themselves in fasting and prayer, and such an extraordinary blessing came to me thereupon, as it is not fit to be repeated.

Ibidem.

Chap. IX.

Of Hackets first comming to Wigginton: of his gadding up and downe: and of the designement to have bin executed in the Star-chamber.

Edmond Coppinger, having thus proceeded in the course you have heard of, at the length hee did send againe for Hacket: the spirit (as it seemeth) moving Hacket, before, to stay at home. Marry now, hee straightly urgeth him to bee at London, three or foure dayes before the beginning of Trinity terme: which he could not be, but came up the first day of the Terme, which was the fourth of June 1591. and lodged at Islington. The day following, hee went to the Counter and there dined with Wigginton, and after dinner hee beganne his Pageant, viz. to cry out against certaine of her Majesties most Honorable privy Councell, and to utter against them most villanous speeches. The next day being *Sunday*, he went to have heard Master *Phillipps preach*: but hee preached not that day there; as the Sexton informed him. Then *hee went*

Cop.to Hac.

Hackets discourse written by Coppinger. 4. Iun.1591.

160. *English Scottizing, for Discipline by force.* Book 4.

to have heard Maister Couper: but seeing a surpless lie there, he departed thence, and went to Master Egertons Sermon. At night *not knowing where to lie, he went to* Wigginton, *where he met with* Coppinger, *and by* Wiggintons *appointment, he lodged at* Master Lawsons. The next morning, viz. the seventh of *June*, hee proceeded with his slanderous out-cries against the said Honourable Councellors; and so continued two dayes after: In the one of which two dayes, hee *was commanded (as is set downe) to goe out of* Pauls *by London gate, and say,* By your leave London; *because he knew he was shortly to remove his dwelling.* The same day also in the forenoone, hee went to the Fleete, to have spoken with Master *Cartwright*: but missing of his purpose, hee left his message with the porter, viz. *that* Master *Cartwright should deale faithfully in the Lords businesse, &c.* Of his afternoones worke, thus it is also in the same place recorded. *He was commanded to sit that afternoone at* Master Lawsons *shop: but the purpose of the Lord in that, and what some of the Citizens themselves know,(he saith) I forebeare to speake.* These courses held by *Hacket*, in the streets, of exclaiming against such persons, &c. did proceede (as it seemeth) by the advice, or at least by the allowance of *Wigginton*, For it appeareth under his owne hand, that hee approved (after his fashion) such out-cryes in the streets to bee lawfull, by two examples: *one out of* Josephus, *and another of a Yorkeshire man, that heretofore had used the like in* London, *as* Wigginton *recordeth.*

Ibidem.

Boman to Wigginton June, 1591.

About this time, viz. in *June*, (as I guesse,) one *John Boman* a servant in *Oundell* did write thus to Master *Wigginton: I desire you to send me a Copy of a writing, which you had from Maister* Cartwright, *upon the Court matters, when Goodman* Hacket *was with you the first time.*

Also, shortly after the aforesaid out-cryes were finished, and

Book 4. *English Scottizing, for Discipline by force.* 161

and many other things thought upon amongst them, (you may beesure to such seditious purposes:) the end of *Trinity* Terme drew neare, when it was commonly expected, that *Cartwright* and the other Ministers in prison, should have come to their answer openly in the *Starre-chamber*. Whereupon a Letter was written by *Coppinger* to his most deare friend *Thomas Lancaster*, the Schoolemaster; from whom hee could keepe nothing that *Lancaster* in policy would suffer to be told him. Which Letter *Lancaster* saith hee did teare in peeces, but confesseth, under his hand, that in the same these words were contained: viz. *If our Preachers in prison doe appeare to morrow in the Star-chamber, and our great men deale with them so as it is thought they will: If God doe not throw some fearfull judgement amongst them, so as some of the chiefe of them goe not alive out of the place, then never give credite to me in any thing, whilest you live.* But Master *Cartwright* and the rest appeared not this day: and so the parties threatned escaped this judgement.

24. Ju. 1591

Chap. X.

A preparation towards the intended disloyalty. Two of Coppin. *Letters to Maister* Chark, *and to another.* Cartwrights *and* Wiggintons *commendation of Penries being then in London.*

Not long after this time, (if not before) Master *Wigginton* and *Coppinger* were very busie, for the better preparing of the peoples mindes, to the readier acceptation of their further purposes, to publish in print two pamphlets of *Wiggintons* pen-

Wigg. ex.

penning, as hee himselfe confesseth. The one was of Predestination, as though (by the abuse of that Doctrine) they meant to have had the blame of all the wicked and intended mischiefes, both of themselves and of their partakers, removed from themselves, and laid upon the Lords shoulders; as though hee should have moved them to such lewd attempts. The other was a kinde of *Ballad*, directed for advice to a young courtier; wherein they make way (as it seemeth) for their friend *Hacket*, and that with wonderfull quotation of Scriptures. I will trouble you onely with foure of the verses.

A Christian true, although he be a clowne,
May teach a King to weare Scepter and Crowne.

And after:
For God will sure confound such as devise
His ordinance or Church to tyrannise.

To these rimes, both for manner and matter, I may well resemble those, made (I doubt not) by the same spirit.

Epi. to Mar. Epistone.

Either from countrey or Court,
Martin Mar-Prelate will do you hurt.

Now that *Coppinger* was a dealer in these things, with *Wigginton* before they were printed, it appeareth by these *Hack. decla.* words of *Hackets* in his last declaration to Maister *Young*: *Wiggintons boy can declare all his Maisters writings; for the boy and Maister* Coppinger *sate writing halfe a night by this examinates bed side, but what they writ hee cannot tell, but one word he heard*, that the Countrey Clowne, can teach the King to weare the Crowne.

After-

Book 4.   *English Scottizing, for Discipline by force.*   163

Afterwards (as I take it) viz. the 9. of *July*, being friday M. *Charke* preached at the blacke Fryers, at which Sermon *Coppinger* was present, who misliking (as it seemeth) some words then uttered, did write a letter presently to Master *Charke*; wherein amongst other points hee saith, *Right reverend Sir, &c. I do not denye (good Sir) but I have now a long time taken a strange and extraordinary course, but such as hath offered occasion of suspicion of my not onely doing hurt to my selfe, but also to the best sort of men now in question, and to the cause it selfe. But by what warrant I have done this, that is all. For if the holy Ghost hath beene my warrant, and carrieth mee into such actions as are differing from other mens, &c. what flesh and bloud dare speake against it? &c. Forbear to censure me and such other, as should deale extraordinarily with me, in the Lords businesse, committed to our charge, and judge of us by the effects which follow; which if you hereafter see to bee wonderfull great, then let all ordinary men call themselves to an examination, &c.* And after, *The waste of the Church cannot be denied to be great, so that there is a place for extraordinary men, &c.* Againe, *my desire heretofore hath beene to have had counsell and direction, but now by comfortable experience I finde, that the action which the Lord hath drawn me into is his owne, and he will direct it himselfe by the holy Ghost, &c.* To conclude, *I beseech you* (saith hee) *to shew this letter to M. Travers and M. Egerton.*

M. Charke upon the receipt of this letter, preaching againe the *Sunday* after in the same place, uttered in his Sermon these words which (*Coppinger* saith) were meant of him, in respect of his foresaid letter, *there are some persons so desperate, that they would willingly thrust themselves upon the rockes of the Land.* This also appeareth by an another letter concerning this second Sermon, written about the 13. or 14. of *July*, to another preacher in *London*, but hee is not named

Cop. to Cha. 9. July 1591.

Coppin. to a preacher the 13. or 14. of July.

med, it had beene to good purpose if hee had beene named: For it seemeth he was as throughly acquainted with *Coppinger* and his fellowes defignements, as it may be wel fuppofed that *Wigginton* was.

In my letter unto *Charke* I manifefted my felfe to have an extraordinary calling, and fignified that the Lord had fo called others befides my felfe, who would approve our felves to bee the fervants of the Lord in a high calling. Againe, the ship (that is the Church) had perifhed, if the Lord had not immediately called three of us to helpe to recover it: &c. My calling is efpecially to deale with Magiftrates; another hath to doe with Minifters, who hath written a letter to you of the City, &c. The third is the chiefe who can neither write nor read, fo, that he is the executioner of the Lords moft holy will: He further offereth to acquaint this Minifter with their whole courfe, and willeth him to fhew this letter to his brethren, and to publifh it where ever he fhould goe.

Hac. laft exc.   *Hacket* confeffed that being about this time (as I take it) with *Wigginton*, the faid *Wigginton* affirmed, in the prefence of two gentlemen and others, *that if the Magiftrates did not governe well, the people might draw themfelves together and to fee a reformation.*

Upon the 15. day of *July*, *Coppinger* and *Arthington* did write a joynt letter of purpofe to have drawne *Lancafter* unto them for the making up of a quaternion. And this was one perfwafion; *If I Ed. Coppinger do not preferre you before any one man in the land whofoever, for your wife, holy, loving, and religious courfe, both in the generall calling o a Chriftian, and in your particular calling, the Lord confound me.*

After *Lancafter* had received this letter, notwithftanding he writ unto him of fome miflike he had of their proceedings, yet (as *Hacket* faith,) hee came unto them all three

the

Book 4.   English Scottizing. for Discipline by force.   165

the same night, to one *Walkers* house at broken wharfe, where they conferred together about an hower after supper. Of what great account this *Lancaster* and some others were with these companions, it doth further appeare by that which followeth. The same day in the morning that *Coppinger* and *Arthington* made their seditious Proclamation in *Cheapside*; they two together first, and afterward *Hacket*, came unto *Wigginton*, and amongst many things, (as *Wigginton* himselfe confesseth,) they told him that M. Cartwright had done *more against Antichrist then any in the world before him since the Apostles times*; and that Wigginton *was comparable unto him, and that* M. Lancaster *was above them both in the estate of heavenly glory, because he had kept himselfe undefiled from the common corruptions of these times, and had a most simple heart to God*. Likewise also they said to *Wigginton* at the same time, that *Reformation and the Lords Discipline should now forthwith be established: and therefore charged* Wigginton, *in the Lords name, to put all Christians in comfort, that they should see a joyfull alteration in the state of Church government shortly*.

Arthington after being examined said, that *Penry* had sent him word by a letter out of *Scotland*, that *reformation must shortly be erected in England: and that he took him (in so writing) to be a true Prophet*. It is not also unlikely, but that *Penry* was a provoker of these men to such their outrages; hoping, that upon their out-cryes and proclamations the people would have risen. For *he was then in London* to have played his part if their attempts had found the good successe they looked for. Marry when hee saw *Hacket* executed, he presently (the same day) posted backe againe towards *Scotland*.

Hac.ex.21. of July.

16. of July.

Jenk.Joh.

Y 3   Chap.

Chap. XI.

Of the trayterous intendments which were towards the Court.

Before this their intended insurrection, it is to be further remembred unto you what was disclosed amongst themselves in their owne discourses and prophesies, (as since it appeareth,) concerning the meanes, whereby they thought to have prevailed, for their Discipline, &c. by those their most lewd, seditious and trayterous attempts. Her Majesties course held for the maintenance of the present government of the Church, was their chiefe griefe: (which course they termed *the defence of abomination: the bearing of the beasts marke, the thrusting of Jesus Christ out of his own rule and government*) and the arraignement of some, with the imprisonment of Cartwright and others.

If the *Star-chamber* day (before mentioned) had held some of her Majesties most honourable privie Councell (whom they supposed to stand most in their light) should never have departed thence alive. After that plot failing, they devised how by their imprecations and cursing of themselves they might perswade the people, that certaine of the Lords of the said most *honourable Councell* were traytors. Wherein how they prevailed I know not, but this I find, that they had not onely *determined to have removed them al from her Majesty*, and to have *placed others in their roomes*, (whom they had already named particularly,) but likewise to have proceeded against their LL. with very hard censures. *The Lord pardon their soules,* (saith Coppinger *for in*

their

Arthington's prophesies.

Udall &c.

Coppinger and others.

Book 4. *English Scottizing, for Discipline by force.* 167
their outward man, they must be punished, though they repent.

Nay in their owne conceits, they had likewise already deprived some of the chiefe of their LL. from their great places of honor, so as when they tooke occasion, to speake seditiously of them, they used their bare names, without any of the honourable titles belonging unto them; as such a man *lately such an officer, Chancellor or Treasurer, &c.*

Besides (when the time of their said intended insurrection grew nigh,) they sent to have her Majesty moved for the committing of her said Councellors; lest in the uprores which they meant to stirre, their LL. might have beene violently surprised, &c. they having peradventure some purpose to bring them afterwards to some of their own more publike courts of justice. *I do advise* (saith Coppinger) *that every one of her Councell, be commanded to keepe their house or chamber for feare of stir and danger; and that such and such, &c. be appointed to waite upon her : and that Maister Wigginton* (*in more favour with God then any man of his calling whosoever,*) *be commanded to be neare her* Highnesse, *to pray to God, and to preach privatly, &c.* [Ibid.]

But that which is especially most horrible, although they might seeme by this last provision for her Majesty, to have indeed some good regard of her safety, yet is it confessed to have bin affirmed amongst them, *that her Highnesse was worthy to be deprived, for giving credit and countenance to the Bishops and such other wicked persons, and for misusing her good subjects*; I thinke they meant the imprisonment of Cartwright and the rest. [Arthin. exa. 19. of July.]

It is also further confessed by *Arthington*, that his fellowes *refused to pray for her Majesty* : and in his second examination hee acknowledgeth, that *hee verily thinketh that* Hacket *meant her Majesty should have beene deprived* : and in his long *Apology* unto the LL. thus : *In my conscience* Hacket

168 *English Scottizing, for Discipline by force.* Book 4.

ket meant to murther those Noble men, that hindered his purpose one way or other, &c. and after, &c. to have done that which my heart and hand for trembling cannot expresse.

Agreeable hereunto are *Hackets* words, both before hee was condemned, and after. *If* (saith hee) Coppinger, *one* Catiline *late of Oundell, and Wigginton were straitly examined, they could utter and declare matters of treason.* And at another time, *If these fellowes* (meaning Coppinger *and* Wigginton, &c.) *were wel sifted, they could declare al the treasons.* And the morning before his death: *It was a gracious and an happy turne, that these treasons were in time revealed: for otherwise it would have cost a number of innocent men their bloud: but now I trust in God that they will reveale their treasons* And thus you see the end and drift of the foresaid extraordinary callings, for the setting up and establishing of the pretended holy Discipline.

Hack. on the torture.
Hack. examined.14.July.

Hack. to M. Yong in presence of di- verse.

Chap. XII.

That of long time some such attempts as Hacket *made for Discipline, were of great likely-hood purposed.*

M Y purpose was not from the beginning either to set downe, or to prosecute the full history of these desperate Reformers, (which is most effectually performed already by another,) otherwise then they doe concerne some other persons, and especially those, not of the meanest of our *Disciplinarian* Ministers, and are thereby very pertinent (in my opinion) to shew the point I have in hand, of the brethrens imitation of the *Scottish* Ministers reformation. For I trust (as I said in the entrance to this part,) it will not now bee denied but that great and many threatning speeches are published:

Conspiracy for Discipline

One

One telleth us, *that great troubles will come of it, if the brethren may not be suffered* to do what they list : another, *that they can no longer endure to be used as they are:* another in effect, *that our Bishops shall be used as they were in Scotland: and that there are moe* of this confederacy *then can be suppressed:* another, *that it is more then time for the hottest brethren to set up the Discipline themselves, without any further staying for Parliaments:* a Synod, *that the people being first instructed, are then to bee thrust into the publike practise of the Discipline:* another man, *that seeing the brethren cannot obtain their wils, by sute nor dispute, the multitude and people must work the feat:* another, *that inferiour Magistrates, of their owne authority within their limits, are to make this new reformation:* another, *that it is a shame for all the favorers of this faction, in that for feare of disturbing of our state, (forsooth,) and offending of her Majesty, they had not before this time cast out our Bishops :* another, *that there are a hundred thousand of this brotherhood in England, who if they come with a Petition for the Discipline to her Majesty, cannot in policie be rejected without danger :* another, *that approved and worthy men of every shire have already consented to this Discipline : that the Eldership is at hand : that the people are inflamed with Zeale, and that it is impossible to stand against it:* another, *that there is a devise amongst them, how to obteine their desires all in one day:* another, *that Bishops are to be packing after the Fryers and Monkes :* another, *that they will have their discipline in spight of all the adversaries of it :* another, *that it is dangerous to the state, if they have not their wils, in regard of the discontentment which will ensue thereby in the hearts of her Majesties subjects :* another in effect, *that the Discipline is like to come into our Church by such a meanes, as will make all the Bishops hearts to ake :* and another, *that he is of this minde, that reformation will not be had without bloud.*

Now

Now if any man, to extenuate these things, shall say: Let every man beare his owne burthen, and be charged with his owne particular actions: what some in the heat of their zeale have published, it ought to have a charitable construction, and cannot well bee further extended to touch any other: as if all the Factioners had entred into such a seditious conspiracie, as the said threatning speeches do import? I answer, that some indeed there bee that do cast these and such like colours over this matter, to bleare mens eyes withall. Some commend their zeale, but not their discretion: some allow their matter, but not their manner: and some will take upon them to excuse both: but as yet I never heard any of that crue, but hee would either in one respect or other, finde some occasion to commend the worst of them.

Besides, where so many of any one sect do concurre in their writings about any new point, it is commonly taken to bee the judgement of them all. And who knoweth not, that if *Cartwright* and the rest had not secretly clapped such fellowes on the backs for their zeale, and laughed in their sleeves to see them go so forward, but had disliked them: his earnest reproofe of the first (being their *Apostle* and *Worthy*) would have prevented all the others that followed, being his *Disciples*. But if it be true, (that I have heard reported) that upon the comming forth of *Martins* Epistle, M. *Cartwright* should say: *seeing the Bishops would take no warning, it is no matter that they are thus handled:* Surely those words from him were enough to set these men agogge. So as that which is commonly reported of great robberies may fitly serve to satisfie the bowlsterers of such lewdnesse.

There are (say they) in such attempts not onely executioners, but also setters, receivers, and favourers: and in
matters

matters of treason concealers, who are all of them within the danger and compasse of law. How this may be applied, I leave it to any reasonable mans consideration, that shall bee pleased to weigh the premisses; aswell considering the said threatning speeches and great bragges, as also the course which was held by the Ministers in prison, and those of the *London fraternity*, together with some others touching the attempts which *Coppinger* and his fellowes took upon them to effect.

Chap. XIII.

Briefe collections, whereby it may summarily appeare, that certaine Ministers in London did know what Coppinger intended.

Igginton (as you have heard) upon *Cartwrights* commitment, &c. writeth *of a bickering, and then a battell to be looked for.* *Coppinger* with his companions *fasteth, and so dreameth of a way how to work wonders* He sendeth *into Scotland concerning an extraordinary calling, signifying that some did fancie to themselves such a manner of calling, who would hazzard their lives, that Christ himselfe, by the abolishing of the Antichristian tyranny,* (which hee affirmed did raigne in our Church,) *might governe in his owne Kingdome.* Wigginton afterward *approveth the lawfulnesse of such a calling in these dayes, our Churches lying waste, &c.* Coppinger & Wigginton with some others, *do thereupon fast againe, to know which of them should be so called.* The lot (forsooth) falling upon *Coppinger* chiefly, he is not silent: but Master *Wentworth* (amongst others)

Z 2 must

must be of his privie Councell. Hee also disclosed himselfe, (after a sort) as you have heard, *to certaine of the Ministers in London* before mentioned: and namely *to Master Cartwright, imparting unto him his severall callings to an extraordinary course for the Discipline, &c. His said writings into Scotland, and Wiggintons said approbation of an extraordinary calling.* He sent Master *Cartwright* the same propositions that *Wigginton* had allowed: whereof Master *Cartwright* afterwards thought there might be good use: he signified unto him, *that by his calling, he was to take in hand such businesse, as in the eyes of flesh and bloud, was likely to bring great danger to himselfe, and unlikely to bring any good successe to the Church*: he told him, *that if he had not beene discouraged, he had before that day procured the release of some that stood then in danger of their lives;* meaning (as I suppose) *Udall*, and *Newman, &c.*

As he dealt with *Cartwright*, so did he with the other Ministers, and with some of them more plainely, desiring still of them all, both *Cartwright and the rest, and that most instantly, that he might be conferred withall, offering himselfe to be altogether ruled by them, either to proceed (if they thought meet) in his said so dangerous businesse, or otherwise wholy to desist and leave it off.* He also offered to impart *unto them all his designements, as to M. Cartwright, not only in generality what he intended, but also the particular meanes, whereby he purposed to bring the same to passe.* Afterwards when through his acquaintance with *Hacket*, by *Wiggintons* meanes, and other incouragements given him by *another of his lay friends*: and by *Wigginton, &c.* that he grew to be more resolute: he signified the same to *M. Charke*, (not past six dayes before their furie brake forth,) still yet *desiring conference* with him, *Travers, Egerton, Gardiner, Cooper*, and *Philips*.

CHAP

Chap. XIIII.

The cunning dealing of certaine Ministers in London, how notwithstanding they wished Coppingers plot to go forward: yet they might be (if it were possible) without the compasse of law.

Consider I pray you the policie, which the said Ministers (mentioned in the end of the former Chap.) used. They at the beginning, no sooner heard of *Coppingers* conceit of an extraordinary calling, to work such great matters: but by and by, (as men acquainted with the foresaid *Geneva* positions,) they very well knew whereunto that matter tended. And therefore whereas the poore misse-led gentleman would have imparted unto them all his secrets: they started from that point, and refused wholy to take from him any knowledge of them.

They sent him some cold messages of their dislike of his proceedings, (which they after qualified, as it hath beene shewed,) not so much to with-draw him from his lewdnesse, as that thereby, if things fell out amisse, they might have some meanes to cleare themselves, by the testimonies of such their messengers, as *Hockenhull* and others. And touching conference that was also by them denied, and surely upon good and provident reasons: For if thereby they should have yeelded in opinion unto him, they knew it might have brought them into apparent danger. Besides, they were not unlike by sufficient arguments to have disswaded him from such a fantasie: which (as it seemeth) was very farre from their meaning. And lastly, it was almost impossible, but that in their debating

174 *English Scottizing, for Discipline by force.* Book 4.

bating with him of his pretended calling, hee most needs have made some mention of such particulars, as with their owne safety they durst not have concealed, and so that way also his platforme would have beene dashed. The safest way therefore for them, was, not to have any conference at all with him: and that course (for ought I finde) they took, to the hardning of *Coppingers* heart, and his fellowes: and to the great adventuring of all the mischiefes that were intended.

It was not denyed amongst them, (as *Coppinger* saith,) *but that the cause was good, which he desired to be an actor in: but the thing that stuck in their teeth, was this: viz. they thought it impossible that hee should bee fit to intermeddle in it, without the endangering both of himselfe* (as Egerton said,) *and of the great cause which hee would seeme to bee most desirous to further.* Howbeit, though *Egerton* would not take upon him, to approve his *extraordinary* calling, (for feare of himselfe:) yet (for all the said danger) hee thought it no policie greatly to discourage him, when hee qualified his speeches after this sort: viz. *hee would bee loth to quench the spirit of God in Coppinger, or to hinder his zeale.*

Numb. 17.
Deut. 31.
Iosuah 1. 9.

Iosuah was called *extraordinarily* by God himselfe, to cast the enemies of the *Israelites* out of the land of *Canaan*, that they might possesse it. Which example Master *Wentworth* applying to *Coppinger*, and encouraging him, upon advice taken, as the Lord did *Iosuah*: viz. *be bold and of a good courage, feare not to be discouraged, &c.* hee shewed no great mislike of *Coppingers* purposes. Likewise, though Master *Throgmorton*, notwithstanding his conference, (as it seemeth) with *Coppinger*, *Arthington*, and *Hacket*, was not acquainted (as he said,) with *Coppingers* particular platformes: yet in that hee confesseth, *hee had heard some buzzes abroad of a*
sole

sole and singular course intended, and doth not only *advise him to imitate the serpents wisdome*, but saith also, *that in affection and good will hee joyned with him*, it could not otherwise be, but that *Coppinger* was thereby greatly animated.

When *Coppinger* told *Udall* that *certaine unlearned men, then lying hid, would shortly take upon them the defence of the cause*, which hee and his brethren in prison stood for, *and would thereby daunt all their enemies, more then they could*, willing *both him and the rest, thereupon to cheare up themselves, for the day of their redemption was at hand*: I do greatly marvaile, what *Udall* thought to be *Coppingers* meaning.

It might well have stood with M. *Charkes* duty, (seeing *Coppingers* full resolution to enter into some desperate attempt, by vertue of his extraordinary calling,) to have disclosed the same to the State. When hee preached in the *Black-Friers*, to the brotherhood there, about two dayes after his said intelligence of *Coppingers* resolution, and but five or six dayes before their proclamation that *there were some persons so desperate that they would willingly thrust themselves upon the rocks of the Land*, thereby to have disswaded *Coppinger*, (who then was present,) or for what other purpose, I know not: hee should forthwith have acquainted the said rocks also, what boysterous tempests and violent stormes had beene ready to assault them.

In this briefe summary, I omit the rest of *wiggintons* actions, referring you to his fellow *Hackets* judgement, both of him and them: They are so apparent, by that which hath beene said, as they seeme to me, to be past conjectures. And I would with all my heart, that all which hath beene hitherto said of the other Ministers, touching this point, did onely depend upon probabilities. For then charity would binde us to iudge the best. But men may

not

not call *good evill*, nor *darknesse light*, nor treasonable conspiracies Ecclesiasticall policies. Mark them (if it please you) for *disciplinarian practises*: and then bearing that brand, owne them who list, and terme them as you fancie.

Chap. XV.

If Hackets treasons had prevailed for the pretended Discipline, how they might have beene defended by the disciplinary doctrine.

I Am not ignorant, that now, if any of the said Ministers or their favourers were asked how they like of *Coppinger* and his companions proceedings: no men will more eagerly exclaime against them. When *Hacket* with his adherents found themselves prevented, and that they were cut off in the beginning of their race, then (to save their lives) they could confesse their extraordinary purposes, pretended before with teares, with fasting, (with groanes and imprecations, to have proceeded from the spirit of God,) to be nothing else but illusions of Sathan, cruell, bloudy, and trayterous designements. But if they had prevailed, what would have beene said of them then? Surely it is no hard matter to guesse. If *Coppinger, Hacket*, and *Arthington* had murthered two or three of the Lords in the *Star-chamber*, the last day of the said *Trinity Terme*, the *Consistorian* doctrine would easily have defended it: especially if their further intents for the Discipline had thereby succeeded. I will tell you a notable historie to this purpose.

About the yeere 1545. (M. *Calvin* then raigning in the Con-

Consistorie at *Geneva*,) one *Norman Lesly* son to the Earle of *Rothsey*, fell at some jarre with the *Archbishop of S. Andrewes*, then a *Cardinall*, for a *private cause* (saith our *Chronicle* and *Buchanans*) betwixt them two, for his dealing, concerning the burning *of one George Wischart*, (saith the history of the Church of *Scotland*.) Whereupon the said *Norman*, with some of his *partakers, conspired the Cardinals death*, they being the rather animated thereunto, *through the Counsell of some great men of the Realme, that had conceived some deadly hatred against him*. The effecting of which conspiracie proceeded after this sort, as is set downe in the said *Ecclesiasticall history*. The 29. of May 1546. the said *Norman*, with 16 or 17 moe, entred by a wile into the Castle of *S. Andrewes*, (where the *Cardinall* dwelt) early in the morning: and after some course taken for possessing themselves of the Castle, *Norman Lesly, James Melvin, and Peter Carmichaell* got into the *Cardinals* chamber, where finding him set in his chayre, and crying unto them, *I am a Priest, yee will not slay me?* the said *Lesly stroke him first, once or twice, and so did the said Peter. But James Melvin (a man, you may be sure, of nature most gentle and most modest,) perceiving them both in choller, withdrew them, and said: This work and judgement of God, (although it bee secret,) ought to bee done with greater gravity. And presenting unto him the point of the sword, said. Repent thee of thy former wicked life, but especially of the shedding of the bloud, of that notable instrument of God, M. George Wischart, which albeit the flame of fire consumed before men, yet cries it a vengeance upon thee, and we from God are sent to revenge it. For here before my God, I protest that neither the hatred of thy person, the love of thy riches, nor the feare of any trouble, thou couldest have done to mee in particular, moved, or moveth me to strike thee; but onely because thou hast beene and remainest an obstinate enemy against*

A a *Christ*

Christ Jesus and his holy Gospel. And so hee stroke him twice or thrice through with a stog sword, and so hee fell. The Cardinall being thus murthered, they seized upon the Artillery and Munition, wherewith that fortresse was plentifully furnished, and likewise upon the rich hangings, houshold stuffe of all sorts, apparell, Copes, jewels, ornaments of Churches, great store of gold and silver plate, besides no small quantity of treasure in ready coine.

F. Thin, and Buchanan.

Some amongst us in *England*, have laboured very earnestly to qualifie *Coppingers* words, where he said, *that God would throw some fearfull judgement amongst the Lords, so as some the chiefe of them should not go alive out of the place*: as though there had beene no violent course intended by him and his associates, but that (in his fond conceit) hee had imagined, that God himselfe from heaven, should have shewed that judgement, for the deliverance of *Cartwright* and the rest. And in my conscience, one gentleman of good credit, not acquainted at all with the *Consistorian* doctrine, in these and such like matters, thought so in his heart. But here this maske is pluckt from such faces as could not bee ignorant what was meant, in that the same spirit which was in *Coppinger*, speaking before in *James Melvin*, or rather (as I thinke) in *Knox*, and his fellow-ministers, (according to whose humor hee penned that history,) do terme the said cruell murther of the *Cardinall*, to bee the *worke and judgement of God*, and that for the manner of the execution of it. Besides, in the margent of the Book, over against the Stabbers blasphemous words, this note is set downe, viz. *the godly fact and words of James Melvin*. But that which moveth mee most, and for the which I have troubled you with this history, is this: that men are animated to commit the like murthers, and the doctrine thereof is stoutly justified according to the heathenish conceit of a certaine tyrant

Book 4. *English Scottizing, for Discipline by force.* 179

tyrant, whom *Cicero* also (a heathen man, but yet of better judgement) doth confute.

Dionysius having spoiled the Temple of *Proserpina* at *Locris*, of *Jupiter* in *Peloponnesus*, of *Aesculapius* at *Epidaurus*, because *Proserpina* drowned him not as he sayled to *Syracuse*, nor *Jupiter* stroke him in peeces with his thunderbolts, nor *Aesculapius* made an end of him by some long and miserable consumption, both he himselfe, and many others accounted such his sacriledge to bee both just and lawfull. And even so it falleth out, for the murther I speak of. Hee that hath eyes to see let him see. *Cicer. de natura deorum lib. 3.*

After the foresaid Castle was surprised, and the *Cardinall* was murthered, *Lesly* with his company, *Knox* and the rest, kept the same Castle by force against the Governour. But at the last they were compelled to yeeld it up: and being thereupon sent (as prisoners) into *France*, they were (by directions there) committed some of them to the Gallies, and some to other prisons. Howbeit in the end they all escaped with their lives by one means or other, saving the said *James Melvin*, who died in prison; whereupon commeth in this notable *Consistorian* doctrine, borrowed of the said heathenish conclusions. *The hist. of the Church of Scotland.*

This we write, viz. (how all but *Melvin* escaped) *to let the posterities to come understand,* (saith *Knox* and his fellowes) *how potently God wrought, in preserving and delivering of these that had but a small knowledge of his truth, & for the love of the same hazzarded all. That if that either we (now in our dayes,) having greater light, or our posterities, (that shal follow us) shal see a fearfull dispersion of such as oppone themselves to impiety, or take upon them to punish the same, otherwise then lawes of men will permit: if (we say) we or they shall see such left of men, yea as it were despised and punished of God, yet let us not damne the persons that punish vice (and that for just cause:) nor yet de-*

A a 2 *spaire,*

180 *English Scottizing, for Discipline by force.* Book 4.

spaire, but that the same God that dejects (for causes unknowne to us) will raise up againe the persons dejected to his glory, and their comfort.

Againe, if our said seditious persons had prevailed with the multitude, (in their other plot) concerning their purposes of removing some of her Majesties most honourable *Privie Councell*, from her service in that place: and in appointing others to succeed them,(whom they fancied to be favourers of their Discipline:) you should have heard (I warrant you) no cries of the brotherhood, nor complaints in your streets, of any of that faction. It would have beene said, as *Goodman* taught at *Geneva*, that, seeing the said *Councellors were enemies to Christs Kingdome, and did seduce her Majestie now, that God had raised them up an* Othoniel *or a* Jonathan *to assist them*, why should they not have joyned themselves unto him? Oh (would some have said) *the holy Discipline, the holy Discipline, the holy Discipline! what Prince or Potentate may resist the holy Discipline and prosper?* Others. *See the hand of the Lord, when men do faile what God can do.* Others, *the greatest works that ever were done in the behalfe of the Church, have beene brought to passe by the basest meanes.* Others, *this is the work of God, and it is admirable in our eyes.* Others, *thus* Josuah *being extraordinarily strengthned by God, threw thirty Kings out of the land of Canaan.* Others, *sufficient warning was given*, and what would they have had men to have done? Then should you have had such a declaration, or proclamation, as you have before heard of; penned (no doubt) by some of the *Consistorian Ministers in Scotland: viz. of the just and necessary causes, moving them and their assistants her Majesties faithfull subjects, to repaire to her Majesty, for resisting of the present dangers, appearing to Gods true religion and professors thereof, &c. and to seek redresse and reformation of abuses, removing from her Majesty, the chiefe authors thereof, &c.*

Declaration 1582. before mentioned.

that

Book 4.   *English Scottizing, for Discipline by force.*   181

that with common consent, redresse and remedy might be provided: Or termed. *The repairing towards Greenwich to the Qu. Majesty*, as elsewhere such attempts have beene coloured.

Likewise, if yet things had not squared to their likings, and that they had gone further with good successe in any violent course against her Majesty, (as it is confessed they purposed to have done,) then also the *Geneva divinity* must have borne the brunt, for the justification of such extraordinary judgements of God. And thus you should have had these matters smoothed over, as partly it may appeare by the assault mentioned at *Sterling*, wherein the King was present in person: and partly by the *Consistorian* propositions, (before set down) touching this point, with many other things, both to bee noted in the premisses, and also in those books, out of the which the said propositions are drawne. [Proclamatiō at Sterling. 1585. F. Thyn.]

I will not trouble you any further with *Ifs*, although I could adde, that if the said traitors had proceeded on forward with their confessed purposes, to have touched her Majesties estate, there wanteth no lesse defence by *Disciplinarian* learning for such a matter, then for the premisses. You may remember the seditious and intolerable propositions before mentioned, as they are truly collected out of our owne countrey mens books, infected at *Geneva* with that pestilent doctrine. Many examples also would have beene brought for that purpose out of *Buchanan, Beza, Knox*, and the rest of that humor; especially the grave resolution given by *Knox* and *Wollock*, generally against all Princes, but particularly then urged and effected by the deposing of the King of *Scots* grandmother from her civill government of that land. And peradventure a part of the said *Knox* his exhortation to *England* written from *Geneva* the twelfth of *January* 1559. (as soone as he heard of her Majesties possession of the royall Crowne of this Realm,) would have beene justified: where [Histo. of the Church of Scotland. pa. 372.373. Exhort. pag. 91.92.]

Aa 3   he

he saith, that *no power nor liberty ought to bee permitted to any state, degree, or authority, (whatsoever they be:) to live without the yoke of Discipline, &c. and that if Prince, King, or Emperour, would enterprise to change or disanull the same, he ought to be reputed an enemy to God, and therefore unworthy to raigne above his people.*

And thus you see how all these treasons, if they had happened, with what *Consistorian* zeale they might have beene defended afterward by the *Disciplinarian* doctrine, which hath beene sent abroad into this Iland from *Geneva*; and meetly well practised already, in some parts thereof by men of that stamp. Whereupon I do collect (the premisses considered) by *Cartwright* and other the Ministers intelligence, with *Coppingers* desperate purposes, that they cared not what mischiefes had ensued, so they themselves might have beene safe. For (as it is most evident by the threatning speeches before mentioned,) there is nothing more laboured for, amongst that sect, then to thrust their many thousands, or some of them into some mutiny or bloudy attempt. Their hope was, that upon any such occasion, their chiefe favourers would not cease to solicite her Majestie, (for feare of further trouble) to grant their desires, or (at least) to take some other course for their contentment, then hitherto (in their opinions) there hath beene taken. They knew, that whatsoever either could or should fall out, under the pretence of seeking for Christs Kingdome, and for the extirpation of the present government of our Church (termed by them to bee so *abominable* and *Antichristian*,) if it had good successe for their devised platformes, yet the said *Consistorian* examples, with their *Allobrogicall* new learning, would have borne it out sufficiently, and maintained it. I pray God deliver *England* from these and such like points of *Discipline*.

For mine owne part, I would not have urged matters in this

this sort, were it not, that I thinke (in my conscience) it is more than high time, that her Majesties faithfull subjects should learne to know these practises, and withall to beware of such Sectaries, as (under their many, both godly and goodly pretences) do thus seditiously endevour to disturbe the land. And the rather also I did it, because I see there are diverse that will needs hood-winke themselves, and stop their eares, with the Serpent in the *Psalme*, of purpose, because they would gladly have these things smoothered up. For hereby it will be apparent to our posterity, that if any such mischiefes, (which God forbid) shall happen hereafter, they were sufficiently warned, that both should and might (in good time) have prevented them, and withall it would then be found true which *Livie* saith: *urgentibus rempublicam fa-* Lib.5.dec.1 *tis, Dei & hominum salutares admonitiones spernuntur*. When the Lord for the sinnes of the people, is purposed to punish any Countrey, hee blindeth the eyes of the wise, so as they shall either neglect, or not perceive those ordinary meanes for the safety thereof, which very simple men, (or babes in a manner) did easily foresee. Which judgement I pray God turne farre away, and long from this and all other true Christian lands and Kingdomes. Amen.

FINIS.